To

Manus

and Back

Sylvester Kapocius

Cover design by Sylvester Kapocius

Printed in Century 11 pt.

Contents

ACKNOWLEDGMENTS

My most powerful driver for writing this book is my wife. She promised to never interrupt me during my writing. She kept that promise, leaving me an open road. What could be better than that? It was a huge, laborious job.

The happy memories of buddies that served with me in the Navy also gave me encouragement to write. The military training that fortified my thoughts also gets recognized.

My buddy Paul Mahan, who wrote of his experiences serving in the Navy, encouraged my thinking to write.

The few reunions I attended braced my thinking to write. Conversations there with all my remaining Navy buddies brought memories to mind which I include in the book.

Last but not least was the support I received from the New Lenox Writers' Group. It allowed me to participate for two years as if I went to school. Their boundless, kindly assistance pulled me through my first attempt to write.

The writings in the book by itself will identify how close I was with all the incidents which occurred during my thirty months in the Navy during World War Two. I thank all those who are a part of my story, "To Manus and Back."

EDITOR'S NOTE

I was honored when Sylvester Kapocius (or Lenny, as I call him) asked me to review his stories. I had witnessed his journey in becoming a writer as he told his stories from World War Two, and developed a deep admiration for him as a person. To get a chance to edit those stories was both a great honor and a huge responsibility.

To me, the most important task was preserving Lenny's voice in telling the stories. He conveys his experiences not just from the first-person but from the heart, a very personal perspective that rings true in every word. His word choices and the way he turns a phrase are truly unique, and I did not want to compromise that. Rather, I wanted every reader to finish this book feeling like Lenny had personally told them this story.

Most importantly, I hope the reader can better appreciate stories from a very important part of history, told by a man who experienced it firsthand. The heroism of him and his many buddies should never be forgotten.

James Pressler

Introduction

This book contains the story of my actual Navy trip as noted in the title. To Manus and Back begins with the attack on Pearl Harbor.

I was sworn into the Navy on July 1, 1943 and was discharged on February 17, 1946.

I did boot training at Farragut, Idaho and more training at San Bruno, California.

I spent 27 months away from home with twenty and one-half months working in the Admiralty Islands, mostly on Manus, serving ammunition to vessels preparing to enter the battle zones.

Manus is located two degrees below the equator and about 300 miles northeast of New Guinea. The climate is very moist and the temperature averages about 115 degrees for the year.

Material for my story has been gathered mostly from my scrapbook, some searches on my computer, and to my amazement, much from memory.

It is a military story which was a difficult part of my life, but I am very proud of it and want to share it with others.

High School (1938-1942)

During those school years, the teachers and we students had our minds on the war, which began affecting our lives. Everyone I knew had a positive attitude to support the troops overseas and was very conscious of the fact that we would also be entering the military service soon. Many of the teachers, doctors, nurses and some clergy left their duties at home to perform their services by entering the military. Chaplains worked closely with the Red Cross. Soon, many supplies dwindled on the home front.

War bonds were advertised and sold for $18.75 with a redemption value in ten years for $25. Stamps were also sold and saved for the chance of purchasing a bond.

At school, there was an Advertising Club directed by one of our drawing teachers. Those who he selected could join with good grades. The members worked with layout of art and learned to do silk-screen setup and printing. One of the outstanding projects was printing decorations on packaged Goodie boxes filled with cookies, cigarettes and personal items donated by the public and shipped to those at the battlefront. I, along with six members of our group, took pride in that project, which we knew was for a good cause. The school's sports events were also printed, and some families near the school asked for printed signs saying, "Stay Off the Grass." With that, they offered a small token which was used to buy supplies for the club.

In my second year of school, 1939, much talk went on of how proud people were to have some family member in the military. Our auto shop teacher was one of them. It was not long until news came of his some being missing in action. How fast this father's mood changed, so significantly and so solemn.

Lifestyle Changes

Soon, life at home became more difficult. All the communities set up an Office of Price Administration (OPA) to control fair prices and to ration and regulate supplies direly needed for the military. A person would have to show positive need at the OPA for a rationed item and receive a ticket for the purchase of it. Doing critical work for the war effort usually provided easier access to rationed items. Stamps were supplied and turned in with the purchase of an item at the store. Business owners had to keep record of purchases carefully. Any person owning an auto could receive a stamp a week for the purchase of only three gallons of gas. Many would save stamps for a longer trip from home. Car pools began, and it worked very well for working people. Maintenance also became a problem; no more replacement parts were manufactured. Public transportation was the way to go. Buses, trains, and street cars were always overcrowded. Many had to wrestle with their schedules. Buses broke down, trains were late, and that's the way it was.

Most manufacturers had to switch to war production in order to survive. Vendors who did not register their inventory accurately and were caught paid a dear fine. Plenty of black-market sales took place in some areas of the city all the way until the end of the war. The shortage of food and certain items became a bit troublesome.

Example: A venetian blind manufacturer switched over to

making boxes for shipment of ammunition. Autos and trucks were no longer made for the general public. Vehicles of all types were built for the military. Chemicals, glass, and paint factories worked day and night along with all the other producers of war goods.

Daylight Savings Time remained without change during the war years. Beneficial to some and troublesome to others.

Scrap metal was in great demand. Old tires were turned into the OPA. The public was asked to save and turn in used cooking grease, as it was an important ingredient in making ammunition and explosives.

People in almost every household started a Victory Garden. This was easy, being just after a recession. Many felt it to be a good idea. It caught on very quickly, not only raising vegetables and fruits but also chickens and rabbits, and trading goods with each other to make their living easier.

The stock market was stable on account of price administration having control of pricing practices. Many owners placed their businesses for sale and very few houses were constructed. Many homeowners remodeled their attics into dormitories and rented them. It attracted those unemployed looking for better jobs and better pay who were willing to relocate to areas where many of the busy defense industries were booming. Everyone was busy and the crime rate was down so very much, and it was noticeable.

We young ones at that time had a chance to make some small change to enjoy. Since all the adults were busy working a lot of overtime, they had no time for their required chores. Occasionally, we were summoned by a whistle down the street to run an errand, help with repairs, paint, or mow a lawn. I'd earn a dime for a trip to the drug store. I found a job, replacing a newspaper delivery boy on a local route. I delivered 108 papers each morning, from five to seven a.m., five days a week, and was paid two dollars, which helped me pay back Mom who lent me money to buy a bike. That bike accrued many miles before it entered the grave. Taller boys took jobs as caddies at golf courses and some stronger boys worked in food stores or on farms. Grocers hired boys to deliver groceries to homes.

The Civilian Conservation Corps

When I was ten, in 1935, employment throughout the country was just about nil. Students graduating school seemed to be loafers in all neighborhoods. Time was aplenty, with nothing to do and no money. Most of the hangouts were in the parks or the streets.

Our government then started a program named the Civilian Conservation Corps (CCC), as this chapter's title shows. The CCC allowed men to join if they were of an adult age, and physically and mentally fit to do many laborious tasks: plant trees, install highway markers, maintain roadways, landscape parks and government areas, put up historical monuments, and other miscellaneous duties as seen fit to beautify each state. Some of their works are still seen to this day.

Those men lived in military-type quarters in typical military style, khaki uniforms and all. They looked like soldiers. Pay was little – enough to buy some personal items and money to visit back home. At home, parents and friends gathered to hear some of their unusual experiences. When the war began, many were the first to enter the Army. Their basic training and living style taught them to be familiar with the military routine. Many received promotions very quickly.

Ages 17 and 18

Getting my high school diploma was good; now what? There were a bunch of tangled thoughts in my mind, but finding work was a must, and soon. I went out to look each day until a job was found. So I went to the Montgomery Ward store's warehouse, which advertised for a silk-screen printer. It was at 600 W. Grand Avenue in Chicago – quite far from home, but I decided to go and try out for the job anyway.

After an interview, the position was available to me on the condition that their company doctor would okay me for this type of work. I passed the physical. The one item the doctor did check surprised me – the color-blind test. Of course, one had to recognize colors accurately in this type of work, since one worked with colored paints.

I stayed with the job only three months, as it became too difficult for me to push paint through the larger screens with the squeegees. I made good pay, but quit and found a job on the CRI&P rail yard, which was commonly known as the Rock Island railroad and is now the METRA system. I worked in their Signal Engineering office as a tracer-draftsman until entering the Navy.

When I worked at Ward's, it was at this warehouse facility that had buildings on three blocks along the north branch of the Chicago River and employed hundreds of people; mostly women. It served its eight-hundred company stores. One of the buildings was a display factory four stories high with a full basement. It made all the advertising items for all of their stores – signs, posters, banners – and packaged them to be shipped to all their retail centers. Ward's competition was Sears.

Quitting time at each department was staggered, each half hour from three to six p.m. Exiting those company doors at quitting time was like a bull's rush. All those aggressive ladies ran to get a seat on the street car waiting for them. Each car would fill like a sardine can before it took off. The closest transfer point I used was three blocks away and over a bridge, so I and a few others walked it so to not get crushed by the wild mob boarding the street cars.

Back then, it was customary to invite a military person over to the house for a dinner to make him feel wanted, being most were so far from home. Most of the ladies crossing the bridge would drop small, wadded pieces of paper with phone numbers on them to the young sailors below. As each group crossed, the sky filled with those pieces of paper like confetti streaming down to the Coast Guard sailors as they attended their security area and couldn't leave their post. Many areas in the Chicago area were under security watch, as I recall.

Many employers would not hire those of draft age. Some quit school to enlist, which I thought was not a very good idea.

Each evening, people would glue their ears to the radio and listen to the latest news from the war front The Philco, Zenith, and RCA radios had lots of news to broadcast. The most popular time was ten p.m.

Before Entering the Service

My first known war casualty was right on our street, three houses away. Ray enlisted as soon as he became 17 years of age. He could hardly wait for that age and then joined the Navy; requiring his parents' signatures. After his training at boot camp, he came back for a ten-day leave. His uniform seemed to fit him beautifully. He was so proud to show himself in it. He was a very nice lad and a very active boy during his childhood.

When he returned to his assigned base, he was assigned to serve on the *USS Yorktown*, an aircraft carrier. While in action during the Battle of Midway, he was killed. Days later, at about three in the afternoon, I saw this messenger hand Ray's mother an envelope at the door. As she opened it, she immediately began to cry so loud it was head three houses down the street.

In another incident at the corner house, a family also received bad news of their son missing in action. He was a soldier, Johnny, sent to the Philippine Islands and presumed to have been grouped with the enslaved during the Bataan March. He was never heard from, but the family never gave up hoping for his return. Many in that March were either tortured and died or were killed. Some of the information gathered indicated he was a part of this. In his childhood, his hobby was raising white rabbits. Occasionally, he would let us feed them in his backyard.

Also, Cy, the captain of his high school football team,

entered the Navy after two years of college. As an ensign in the Navy, he was assigned a mission in the Pacific. There, he flew with his plane off the deck of an aircraft carrier and never returned. It has never been determined what happened – attacked, lost in bad weather, ran out of fuel, or bad navigation. Many pilots who were trained for a short period of time were called ninety-day-wonders, having had training as pilots for only ninety days.

Another man lost in action was nicknamed Suds. He began college studies after high school, and while in his second year his notice came up to become a part of the military. He was inducted into the Air Force and joined a navigator crew on a B-25 bomber. On a flight to Europe, his flight was lost over the ocean in a huge barrage from an enemy attack.

I remember well when he came home on leave before heading overseas. He surprised his fiancée, who worked at a bakery, by just popping in to see her during his one and only leave. She was so overjoyed with that surprise visit; I can still visualize the look on her face, and him in his brown leather Air Force jacket with the patch signifying the military group he was attached to. When they looked at each other, there had to be only one single thought in both their minds: Love.

Our neighbor, Stan, as a young boy was chicken when it came to rough play in the prairie. When his mom told us he was in the Navy as a male nurse, we could not believe it. When he saw the smallest amount of blood, he actually became pale and almost passed out. Evidently, he did well in his work as a medical corpsman because he was promoted several times during his hitch.

Bally, a bachelor and boozer within the community, had a slight problem. The day he was to report for induction, he went on a binge. The same day, two military personnel showed up and asked about his whereabouts. They found him – yep, drunk as a wet fish with his head hanging over a bar in a local tavern. They hauled him away quickly. Months later, we saw him come home from the service and his looks and behavior appeared to be as a real gentleman.

Many tried different methods to avoid or be deferred from being inducted into the military. Some escaped by leaving the country, some tried to have their family physicians give notice that they were physically not capable to perform the required duties which the military required. Some even did bodily harm to themselves by destroying a limb or even digesting a drink of some sort that would alter the heartbeat at the time of the required physical examination, but they had to report for a re-check in six months.

Many people doing critical jobs in a defense production factory or any job where their loss would interrupt the war effort or hinder safety or security in our country were exempt from military duty. As the war progressed, more troops were needed. Those once deferred were called to serve. Many began to worry. A husband with two children would be called to serve, which worried a lot of people. Husbands with two children were already being taken to serve at the last months of the war.

While I served with them, they spoke of the hardships their families endured. The children missed their father badly, so

13

despondent that they became ill. The Red Cross was notified to intervene, and as a result, the fathers were returned home and discharged from service.

Some men within our group were from Hawaii and Puerto Rico, and went to join the United States Navy. Prisoners with mild sentences could volunteer for service and it replaced their time in prison.

At the LaSalle Street station in Chicago was a sign hanging inside the main entrance that read, "Travelers Aid" with an arrow pointing to the desk in the corner. Most needing help were nervous and lost travelers. Some just needed directions, some had lost items, some were meeting a person at the station, some jilted by a boyfriend, or pregnant or ill passengers needing comfort. All were assisted one way or another by the people at the desk. Financial assistance was also rendered to some.

Travelers filled the bus stations and the railroad terminals, continuously moving from here to there all across the forty-eight states.

Time to Leave Home

As all my buddies were enlisting in one branch of the service or another, I felt it was time for me to move along with them. Without any hint to my folks or the boss at work, I went down to the recruiting station in Chicago on Plymouth Court. When I got there, I was told the agenda was filled for the day. I thought it was not a good idea to take off work again soon, so I waited. After four days, a notice appeared in the mail for me from the Selective Service System to report to my local Draft Board.

This system was established in 1938 by Congress to permit the recruiting of single men, the age of 21 and older, to serve in the armed forces of our military.

Because of the unrest in Europe at the time, our government felt the need for a military defense of our country. As this happened, the 21-year-olds married quickly in order to avoid the draft. In 1939, Hitler entered Poland with his troops. The draft age was then dropped to the age of 18. In all of the communities in our country, Draft Boards were set up to classify men to serve in our country's military. Those excused were only those who were married, some with family hardships, those employed in critical jobs, ones who refused to serve on account of their religious beliefs, and the physically unfit.

At first, when the war broke out, draftees went into the Army. Then the other branches of the military needed men, so if one was able to pass the tests, they were able to join their choice of military service.

Doctors and chaplains were also needed, so many joined without hesitation. While in service, they worked closely with the Red Cross.

Those who were sent through the recruiting station within the Selective Service System by the Draft Board would not be subject to serve in a standard enlistment period of four or six years unless they so desired. The drafted would serve for the duration of the war plus a maximum of six months. It was titled the V-6 Program.

In my case I requested to join the Navy, but did not want to enlist for four or six years, so they assigned me to the USNR-V6 unit of the Navy. This resulted in me serving up to the war's end plus six months.

When the orders came for induction, instructions were given to bring only one change of underclothing and nothing of personal value;

Immediately, I told my employer of the situation and my folks, who became sad. The next morning, the first thing was to check all my valuable belongings. That was funny, as I had none.

While I got on the train to the Induction Center, many thoughts passed very swiftly through my mind. How fast eighteen years had gone by.

As a child I was raised by my Lithuanian parents, both immigrants with little education who raised us quite sternly with their attitudes supporting their beliefs and ways of life. My three older brothers and I were greatly influenced by the examples and actions they presented which carried us into adulthood. We had a very hard-working mother and father. Many duties were placed on us in order to survive during the agonizing Depression. I hated beating the rugs, shoveling coal into the coal bin of the basement twice-yearly, canning foods for the winter, picking up ice with the wagon from the ice house four blocks from our house, cleaning out the septic system in the back yard, and constantly hearing, *do this, do that.*

The worst part was worrying about my father, who earned sixteen dollars per week, supporting us six as a laborer at the factory. He could not lose his job. Jobs were very scarce. Men at factories lined up at the door, hoping to get hired.

When the first Superman comic book came out in 1938, a copy of it getting passed around in the street was a big deal. In a few days it frazzled, and into the garbage it went. Someone in the neighborhood had a *Monopoly* game which many of us enjoyed for many, many hours.

One day when I was eight, at the park swimming pool, my oldest brother threw me in deep water and hollered to me, "Sink or swim!" That did it; my nickname became Sailor. It also became my favorite sport.

We biked many miles to just swim in a clay hole or to a small airport to watch planes take off or land. We all knew how to repair our bicycles.

Sitting on a fire plug near a busy highway was a pastime of ours, counting cars, observing their makes, and hassling about their values. There was a lot of discussion among us about what the future of the auto industry would be. Many said that autos would never reach speeds of 100 miles per hour. Many said a V-type engine would never be produced as it would vibrate too much. The day that hydraulic brakes were installed in autos was a great achievement. Polyfiber tires were developed, which was wonderful as they lasted longer and fewer flats, better than the old rubber one. Vehicles made to last longer, and even better were air bags and safer autos on better-built highways became a plus for the life we have now. So many things first introduced during the war years made our life easier.

The saddest days seen by me were at times seeing those who actually rummaged through food scraps or the expired store items thrown out behind the building.

Signs in red lettering hung in the windows of some homes, saying in large letters, "Quarantine." Below was the reason: Measles, pneumonia, whooping cough, scarlet fever, or some other illness with warning words, "Stay Out. City Health Department."

We junked through prairies looking for scrap to sell to the scrapyard businesses for movie money. In the 1930s, in the south part of Chicago where I lived, a movie cost five cents, four cents for regular gasoline and five cents for premium. At the station, one would have to pump the gasoline manually into his vehicle. Milk was 15 cents per gallon, and at grocery stores, a regular customer was given a gift at Christmas time. If a person spent a dollar or more, they'd receive a pound of pure cooking lard for free.

The future looked so bleak in the late 1920s and early 1930s. One time in that period, a thought entered my mind to just lay out in the street and see what would happen to me. Another idea was to just run away from home, hoping to find a better way of life.

Three of my friends did just that and hopped a freight train going west. Two got as far as Iowa then gave up by lingering on a street in town where the law picked them up. The police then called the parents of those two for money to ship them home. The third got as far as Hollywood, California, and existed on small change doing chores for movie stars. We met years later, and in conversation it appeared to me he chose to live the rest of his life as a bum.

During the Depression, the hard times made people stick with each other with their problems. Both labors and happiness were endured together by all without spending too much money.

Now it was time for me to leave home, and where to and what will happen next is beyond my control – my one and only thought.

From Recruiting Station to Boots

We were sworn in and had to abide by the rules of the United States Navy. Our next move required was basic training at boot camp. From Plymouth Court in Chicago, our group walked through the city's Loop, east on Van Buren Street toward Lake Michigan and settled in Grant Park. Our group numbered three- to four-hundred. We missed lunch and our stomachs surely let us know that. Finally, sandwiches arrived at about 4 p.m. Jibber-jabber went on, discussing our next unknown move. We were told browsing was allowed, but we must report back by 6 p.m. We were also warned of the consequences if we got back late. Since we were now military personnel, we would be considered AWOL – Away Without Official Leave – and would be punished.

Those couple of hours gave me an opportunity to skip over to the LaSalle Street station building where I was employed to say goodbye to my friends for the last time. Upon entering the office, I was asked where I would be shipped out to. I had no answer. All I talked of was what my recruitment day was like. My, how many long lines we had to wait in before being cared for; wait, wait and more waiting. My first dislike of military service.

During my conversation with the office clerk, he asked, "Why is your group not just being loaded on the train and sent to the Great Lakes Naval Training Center boot camp, which is only an hour's ride?" That was a very good question.

That clerk had many dealings with people working in and

around the depot. He said to me, "Let me check around and see if a Rock Island train might be your troop's transportation." After checking, he returned excitedly, informing me that a bunch of empty cars were in the depot, preparing to be loaded soon; about 7 p.m., to transport recruits of *Navy* personnel numbering about what was in our group. He also found the destination was way up in the northern part of Idaho. Never heard of a naval base up there.

Well, the story was this. When World War Two started, they realized that since more men were entering the Navy, there was a need for more training centers. Then-president Franklin Delano Roosevelt decided to cruise with his wife in a special plane to look for a suitable area in the country for construction of a naval base. They finally spotted a large, wooded area on level ground and a body of water for boating. He picked this place in the very far north of Idaho and named it Farragut. Six camps were put up and each was named after men who gave up their lives at the start of the war. Camp Waldron, Camp Bennion, Camp Hill, Camp Peterson, Camp Ward, and Camp Scott. I trained at Camp Ward.

Farragut, Idaho, Here I Come

With rush hour being over in the city, we walked from the park to the train station at LaSalle and Van Buren Streets. It was about a mile. In the depot was this long train with its engine's steam spurting out through the depot's roof opening and the conductor walking beside the train, shouting for us to pick our own car and seat.

A new acquaintance and I hopped on one of the older cars that I knew had sleeping berths. They were older Pullman cars pulled out of their graveyards and cleaned up to be used as troop trains.

When the train pulled out of the depot, its good wooden structure creaked as if in pain because of its old age. As we left the depot, we talked of how exciting it was so far, looking out of the windows as we moved, leaving the city behind.

The first night on the train went by very fast as we slept in a comfortable bunk with white linen bedding. When we awoke, our train was standing idle behind the state capitol building in Jefferson City, Missouri. Now our train faced west. We began to wonder about our first meal of the day. No breakfast, only drinking water from the fountain. Soon the train began to move and scenery became more interesting as we looked out the window. Down the line, we stopped at Eldon and Versailles to pick up new recruits. We only found out years later that those rails we rode on were the last time they were used by a locomotive. Rails can be seen in those two cities, and since there is not enough interest, no section of rail line has reopened since.

Our next stop was Union Station in Kansas City, Missouri. There was lots of action at the depot. A very nice restaurant in the train station building already had meals ready to serve us by the waitress group named Harvey Girls. They gave us jolly welcomes as they served efficiently without a hitch. Our time there was short. The girls waved us goodbye with kisses as we left the depot. When pulling out, we saw an Army troop train on the side track with its large doors open, and soldiers with their feet hanging out. Many were peeling potatoes for the next meal – I guessed.

Starting out of the depot was very fast and the speed remained at a high pace most of the way to our next stop, which was Tucumcari, New Mexico. It was a transfer point onto the Union Pacific from our Rock Island train. Then only coaches were available for the remainder of the trip. No more of those comfortable sleeping berths.

For a short while we headed west, then turned north for the rest of the trip. We began heading for the hills. A large steam engine seen on the side track soon pulled out and hooked up to our train. It took two engines to get to the top of those hills by zig-zagging all the way up. It was the largest steam engine I had ever seen in my life that assisted our train. At the top, the big guy unhooked and left. The one engine now had to keep its brakes applied in order to have control of the train downward with the heavy load. Zig-zagging all the way down, smoke from the brakes was bluish-gray and nauseating as it drifted through the open windows of the train. Finally, after five days and five nights of travel, now riding on level terrain, we entered the city of Sand Point, Idaho. Many buses waited for us at the depot. After a short, fifteen-minute ride on the bus, we were unloaded at the main gate of the naval base for boot training.

Inside the base, we were told to go directly to the large, close building which was the commissary for the new arrivals. In an orderly fashion we received Navy clothing and bedding. Civilian clothes were either to be returned home or destroyed on sight, all of us were told. I sure was happy to receive all new garments, but when sizes were not too fitting and we started complaining, we were told we would grow some and soon would fit into them as time goes by. Well, not in my case. The shoes handed to me were such that when I walked, I stepped twice before my shoes moves once. I had to put three cuffs on my trousers. The shirt made good pajamas, and the underpants had to be pinned for them to stay on.

My seabag was stuffed with clothing. A hammock and a small bag called a ditty bag were then handed to us. Our company number was stamped on each item – mine was 523. With all of this to carry, we were told to walk to our assigned barracks. Mine was Camp Ward, about two blocks away. With our loads, we trudged and stopped repeatedly like penguins on a trail. With all the buildings having two floors, 65 men were put in each. I hauled my load to the top level. I chose the upper bunk, since my bunk partner was a bit taller than me.

As soon as we got situated, those who were smokers headed for the smoking area under a canopy outside the barracks. A lamp would be lit there when smoking was permitted.

Eight p.m. was time for the flag-lowering; a short ceremony

that we attended. A sounding from the camp bugler at 9:55 was the reminder for all the lights to be turned off at 10 p.m. As the lights diminished, the bugler played Taps. A second bugler sounded a few seconds later, heard from the next camp, which became an echo. That's where my reminiscing of home came to mind.

Anyone not respecting the "Be Quiet" rule after Taps was sounded would be punished.

Each person in the company did four-hour guard duties at night outside the barracks at scheduled intervals throughout boot training.

First Night in A Boot Bunk

A shore patrol banner is worn by whoever is assigned guard duty, and patrols inside the barracks during the night hours. In his case, it was the hours from 8 to 12 p.m. Not quite settled down for the night. About ten minutes before sack time, 10 p.m., the guard would shout loudly, "Clear the decks," meaning everyone get in their bunks. Not a single sound would be heard as Taps was played by the bugler outside the barracks. Here and there were heard snorts, sneezes and gas eruptions throughout the room in the dimly lit areas as we began to snooze.

An assigned guard walked outside the periphery of the building. This was done at nights only. Armed with a rifle, if someone approached him, he would shout, "Stop, who goes there?" Then they must identify themselves.

Even though the entire base was under security, if one was not attending to that duty properly, he would be punished. For some, quite severe extra duty would be given to them. It usually gave the message to obey the rules.

Our commander told us that we had to expect a lot of guard duty during our military service, which became so very true.

My first night was strange. So far from home, entirely new surroundings, unaccustomed to new furnishing and sleeping in a bunk. I chose the upper one as my partner was a bit taller than me.

My bunk partner, John, was from Cicero, Illinois. His folks

owned a bicycle store with a repair shop. I asked what he did there, the answer was not much, sat around most of the day. Right from the start of our training he did not care to comply with the commands to perform those very strenuous, continually repeated exercises required of us. He constantly complained of how difficult it was to accept those daily orders and make efforts to strain the body. He bore on my sympathy.

About the fourth day, as we awoke, John says to me, "I can't do this anymore" repeatedly. I told him to sit down on the bunk and rest a while. I went to the chow line for breakfast but he did not go.

When I returned to the barracks, I asked those nearby, "Where is John?"

Two men popped up and said that duty guards restrained him and took him away to Ward 9, the psychiatric ward, as he continued to holler, "I can't do this anymore!" He never returned.

At the end of each day, just before 10 p.m., the bunk was so very enticing. The work-out and the quarantine shots given every ten days made us sick and tired but we had to keep up with the daily routine. Receiving shots required us to line up outside the building where the medical team had a table set up with all the necessary supplies. The corpsmen would inject us one after another in a hurried fashion. Some would pass out as the sun got to them. Needles were washed in alcohol pans and used again. Dull needles occurred from repeated use and we called them "square needles." Those jabbed by a square needle had to be injected with a bit more force by the corpsman, which made some a bit angry. With all the shots making us feel dopey, no energy, and some getting hives as a result, we called it, "Cat fever." Being in such an uncomfortable situation did not excuse anyone from making an effort to perform the daily exercises. It was tough.

I remember the first night after Taps was played, this one joker, Benjy, shouts from his bunk, "I wanna go home," in a crying tone that made us all laugh, and it roused the guard to check on the incident at hand.

A total of 65 men were bunked on both the first and second floors of the barracks. A washroom at the end of the room had dimmed lights to find our way around the fairly dark areas.

Taps

We in the United States have heard the song, Taps. It's the song that gives us the lump in our throats and also tears in our eyes. Do you know the full story behind this song? If not, I think you will be interested to find out about its humble beginnings.

Captain Robert Ellicombe was with his men near Harrison's Landing in Virginia. The Confederate Army was on the other side of the narrow strip of land. During the night, Captain Ellicombe heard the moans of a soldier who lay severely wounded on the field. Not knowing if it was a Union or Confederate soldier, the captain decided to risk his life to bring the man back for medical attention. Crawling on his stomach through gunfire, he pulled this man to camp. Finally reaching his own lines, he discovered it was a Confederate soldier and he was dead. The captain lit a lantern and suddenly caught his breath, then went numb with shock. In the very dim light he saw the face of the soldier. It was his own son. The boy had been studying music in the South when the war broke out. Without telling his father, the boy had enlisted in the Confederate Army.

The following morning, heartbroken, the father asked for permission from his superiors to give his son a full military burial. Despite his enemy status, his request was partially granted. The captain asked if he could have a group of Army band members play a funeral dirge for his son. The request was turned down since the soldier was a Confederate. Out of respect for the father, they said they could give him one musician.

The captain chose a bugler. He asked the bugler to play the series of notes he found on a piece of paper in this dead youth's uniform. His wish was granted. Now the haunting melody we know as Taps, used at military funerals, was born. The words are:

Taps

Day is done
Gone the sun
From the lakes, from the hills, from the sky
All is well
Safely rests
God is nigh, fading light, dims the sight
And a star
Gems the sky
Gleaming light, from afar, drawing nigh, falls the night
Thanks and praise
For our days
Near the sun, neath the skies, this we know
God is nigh

Boot Training

We began our training with a schedule given to us verbally by our commander, who was formerly a physical education teacher. His name was Andriotti, so we nicknamed him Andy. He stood six feet tall, weighed about 170 pounds and was 35 years old. His rank was Chief Petty Officer.

He explained to us what we needed to accomplish after eight weeks of training in order to graduate and then be promoted to a higher rank. Exercise, studying, and many instructions given to us would consist of many things. A Navy Bible was given to us which contained 784 pages. It would be our guide along the way, but had to be studied. The first four weeks we followed through all of the boot camp's training schedule. The second four weeks we followed the same schedule, except with a more aggressive attitude.

At the end of his spiel, he stated his strengthening remark to us. "I do not expect anyone to do anything in training that I cannot do."

The same morning, an hour after our session, the first outdoor exercise began. Guess what it was? Marching, of course! The huge field outside the barracks was called "The Grinder." Stones of one-inch size covered the ground to march on. Squads were formed and the marching began. At once we felt how weak our legs were, even wearing heavy shoes and the legs strapped with patees.

Besides the marching was this list on the training schedule. Cross-country run, commando maneuvers, rope-climbing, hiking, weight lifting, Jujitsu, boxing, wrestling, calisthenics, weapons firing, seamanship practice, and swimming.

When indoors, we practiced signaling, read the Navy Bible, wrote letters to our loved ones, or just gabbed. Suitable weather allowed most of our training outdoors.

At the end of our first week, we were all tested for our swimming abilities. This base had an indoor activities building with a swimming pool. When I got there, I smiled. I like water.

The instructor explained to us: To graduate boot camp, one must pass a swimming test. There were three classes of swimmers. The test for first class would be first.

The first-class type must be able to perform three functions in deep water. First, swim one-hundred feet underwater, allowing once up for air. Next, swimming three different strokes of one's choice. Third, removing a jersey or shirt from the body and tying it to a floatable device while in deep water.

Would you believe only four of us out of 130 in our group, from all over the country, volunteered to be tested for first class? All four of us passed, but I was the slowest.

The four of us came from the Chicago area and together discussed the areas we spent most of our time swimming. Yep, it was Lake Michigan.

Swimmers for the second-class test had to be able to remove

a garment from their body and knot it to a floatable device in deep water. To pass third class, one only had to show he could swim across the width of the pool, which was about 35 feet.

After testing, 40 were not swimmers, but they learned and we all graduated together.

Every evening the recreation and activities building was quite fully occupied with those who used an hour or so to build up their body skills.

In the gymnasium we had to practice rope-climbing, boxing, wrestling, weight lifting, and push-ups. We always began with the famous military Jumping Jack.

Points were totaled on each person's activity. At the end of boot training, we were told of our progress made. All were happy to hear the results on graduation day. I knew my fifty push-ups and swimming helped my score.

I also took a written aptitude test and had a few questions thrown at me by the psycho doctor.

Seamanship schooling took place on the water's edge of Lake Pond O'Reille. We marched quite far from camp to get there. The water was very cold as melting snow from the mountains fed the lake year-round. There we did rigging, boat launching and boating, commando tactics, but the first thing on the list was to learn how to make a square knot.

Graduation Day

It was a beautiful day and I was so proud as all of us were. It was the Sunday before Labor Day. Knowing that I, being up in mountain country felt better also – strange.

At sunrise before chow, our commander came into our barracks to remind us to attend church services at the activities building. All faiths were welcome. Most all of our group attended.

After lunch, many officers with their guests and other dignitaries came into our camp to view the graduating ceremonies taking place. We marched to the Navy's outstanding band's music, so beautiful that I just shuddered, making me feel so proud to be an American.

We were all dressed in white uniforms, together, marching in stride, leaving memories with me to this day. Photographers were very busy taking pictures.

The following day, our entire company gathered on the field's bleachers and were photographed as a group. Each bought a photo for one dollar. The same day, two white stripes were sewn onto the left sleeve of our jersey, signifying the rank of Seaman 2/c. Those having previous experience of a craft coinciding with any Naval services were promoted to higher ranks. The ROTC high school graduates were promoted one rank higher.

Hooray, what a break! A ten-day leave was given to us. Many of us living out east had a Navy bus drive us to Seattle, where we purchased a ticket to ride the train on the rails of the Northern Pacific railway to Chicago. The train moved fast for many hours between station stops. Less than six stops were made for sailors dropped off at their home stations. The steam engines needed water filled into the tender and coal was loaded for fuel. At those stops, fill-ups were done quickly.

It was a boring ride as I saw only barren land while going through that northern part of America, looking through the train window for hours. I wondered how the heck those people up there lived with no visible activity.

When I got home, those eight days of leave went fast. Nothing had changed. Some grumbled about their hardships on account of the war. Their lifestyle was affected. It had to be endured. They learned to live without the usual goodies they were accustomed to. Some of their daily needs were hampered.

No one of draft age was seen anywhere. If someone was seen, it was for some special reason that they were deferred from being in the military.

The day after my leave, I was instructed to report to the information desk in the lobby of Union Station in Chicago at 8 a.m. There I showed my identification and was told to get on the troop train in the depot, which was already being filled with Navy personnel.

Heading West

A mixture of civilians and Navy personnel were on the train. The conductor said we are going way out west. I thought, having grown up in the Great Lakes region and having lived through cold winters, I would be sent to some base or ship on the east coast. That did not happen.

Our sea bags and hammocks were forwarded, so then it was like, "Be ready for the next surprise." We were told to never reveal information to anyone about our moves as we traveled, so our destinations most always were never told to us.

About twelve hours into the journey, our train entered a side track. There, all Navy personnel were told to get on another train waiting for us. It was our ride for the remaining trip.

As usual, our train started out quickly, but soon – in a few hours or so – we got sidetracked for a train having priority carrying military supplies. Next stop, to fill the water tender. Next day, same thing – got sidetracked for another train. Typical for troop trains. We continued to make stops all the way through Iowa, Nebraska, Utah and Nevada.

While crossing the country from east to west, at many stops folks from their communities came to the train with open arms, wishing us well on our long, tiring journey. Some came from remote locations just to see a troop train containing military personnel. Folks from most everywhere had some loved one in the service and was very much conscious of the ongoing war. Some handed out cookies and apples through the windows of the train, some played music, had loud conversations, exchanged names and addressed, but soon the train moved on.

Entering California, our first stop was at a red signal, located right close to a peach orchard. For three sailors in our car, the temptation was so great they jumped out the window, jumped over the farmer's fence, and picked some peaches. Soon, we heard shots ringing through the air from inside the property. The trees hid the shooter, but the message was clear. The train began to move as the three jumped back on just in time.

At about four o'clock, the conductor walked through our car and we hollered, "We had no lunch!"

His reply was, "Very soon, very soon."

Shortly, he returned and handed us each a skimpy sandwich and no drink. We all soon began to grumble. He returned, jingling a few coins in a tin container that he then left in the car. It's considered a starter for expecting a tip for services rendered. When he came back, not only were the coins gone from the container, but the tin can was tossed at him as he made a quick dash to the next car. He was not seen for the remainder of the trip.

About an hour later, a pleasant-appearing conductor with a smiling face entered our car. During a conversation with him, he informed us that Oakland, California, would be our last stop.

San Bruno, California – Tanforan

We finally got off the train at five o'clock at the busy Oakland depot and we were very hungry. I felt strange and also confused. Three Navy buses were there to transport us to our next location. No bus went to a ship; all went to a naval base. The first bus went to Moffet Field, the second to Mare Island, and the bus I was on took us to San Bruno. We cruised right over the Bay Bridge, right through San Francisco, and onto Route 101. We rode on it for twelve miles southward then stopped right smack at the front gate of a horse-racing track.

"Did our bus driver get lost? What the heck are we doing here?" we all remarked. The driver set his brakes, turned to us and shouted, "Okay, guys, this is it, everybody off."

We sang, "Off again, off again."

At the gate stood a Navy shore patrolman. Above him, a sign read, "United States Navy." We formed a line, showed our IDs, and passed on through the gate. We looked around. No horses inside, just Swabbies.

To All Persons of Japanese Ancestry

The Western Defense Command and the Fourth Arm Wartime Civil Control Administration, Presidio of San Francisco, California, was in charge. Signed, J.L. DeWitt, Lt. General, US Army, May 3, 1942

WESTERN DEFENSE COMMAND AND FOURTH ARMY
WARTIME CIVIL CONTROL ADMINISTRATION
Presidio of San Francisco, California
May 3, 1942

INSTRUCTIONS
TO ALL PERSONS OF
JAPANESE
ANCESTRY
Living in the Following Area:

Map of the West Coast Defense department Japanese relocation areas. 100,000 To 200,000 were subject to internment, and about 30,000 escaped internment.

* WCCA Assembly Center   ○ mixed facility
▲ WRA Relocation Center
▢ WRA Isolation Center
▱ WRA Temporary Camp or Other WRA Facility
☆ Justice Dept., U.S. Army, or Other Facility

Office for relocation of the internees.

Transportation by trucks, buses, and rails.

RELOCATED AND ASSIGNED TO LIVE IN THIS AREA WHEN WW-2 STARTED

THIS ARTICLE WAS TAKEN FROM THE NEW LENOX COMMUNITY REPORTER ON 11-04-2015

One of the shacks at Tanforan

Home of Japanese Internees
April 28, 1942
To
October 13, 1942.
Then the U.S.NAVY
moved in.

My Tanforan Home
October 13, 1943
TO
March 27, 1944.
Then boarded
USS SEAFLASHER.

San Bruno, California.
Tanforan
Only one mess hall was operating today.

Spoony, Stovepipe, Ski(Me), and Pete. Jan. 13, 1944.
It was by wash day. It was also the same day
that we all signed our Last Will and Testament.

On February 19, 1942, President Roosevelt signed executive order 9066, which laid the legal foundation for the forced evacuation and imprisonment of Japanese-Americans. None were convicted of charges.

On April 2, 1942, they reported to the Civil Control station in San Francisco. One-hundred-and-eighty thousand were processed, about 120,000 at Tanforan, and then were sent to relocation centers to live. For a large portion, the racetrack in San Bruno was their homestead – about 8,000 between April 28 and October 13, 1942.

Converting Tanforan (My Life There)

During World War Two, Tanforan was used as a Japanese-American internment camp. It was the second-most populous "civilian assembly center" for internees being relocated to a more permanent and remote relocation center. They lived in converted horse stables at the racetrack.

When they were all vacated, each military branch was offered the use of that area as their military base. Because of its deplorable condition, they all refused – except for the Navy.

Twenty-six barracks were built and soon occupied by Navy personnel. The base was then used for advance training and a holding area for transferees.

My group entered in October, 1943. The barracks were already filled to about eighty percent. Those who vacated left a garden of vegetables, still growing but getting trampled on by everyone using that piece of ground for exercises. Autos driving by slowed to watch through the wire fence.

Inside the gate, the first thing seen was an outdoor prison for sailors. It was enclosed by a cyclone fence. Anyone causing a problem was put in there *pronto*. Those imprisoned were fed "P and Punk," meaning water and bread, for three days, then they received a full meal. If someone was isolated for more than five days, they would be transferred to a permanent facility. That cage was never empty. Buddies always found ways to sneak food to them.

DRILL HALL-INDOOR ACTIVITIES

FLAG RAISING

SIGNALMAN SCHOOL

NATATORIUM

STROKING

WHALEBOAT

OUTDOOR RIFLE RANGE

INSIDE BARRACKS

COMPLETE HAMMOCK

COMMANDO COURSE

JAMES RICHARD WARD
LOST ON HIS SHIP,
THE USS OKLAHOMA
WHILE HELPING MEN
AS SHIP SANK AT
PEARL HARBOR ON
DECEMBER 7, 1941.

CAMP WHICH I DID
MY TRAINING AT,
CAMP WARD

Then we were marched over to the mess hall, we ate, and then were directed to our assigned barracks. Those building we slept in were just ugly shacks constructed with thin sheets of plywood, spaced evenly down the rough roadways throughout the

42

camp. Walking down the road, conversations were heard through the buildings' walls. Inside, the floorboards had spaces between them with the ground seen below. Cool air entered through the openings, which made it uncomfortable during some nights. An oil-burning stove was in each building. A single light bulb hung by the cord above the door on each end of the room. The walls quivered when someone slammed the door too vigorously.

It was the rainy season. Once during a ten-day period, a sprinkle continued without stopping. That time was good to catch up with letter-writing, washing clothes, studying lessons for another promotion, playing cards, or just resting. There were no recreation areas on the base.

After three weeks, a group of about thirty torpedo-trained graduates joined us. Many had ratings and hatch marks on their jerseys, indicating they were seasoned sailors. I remember two who brought with them some torpedo juice called Pink Lady. They cut it with Coke and sipped it to get high. We named it Varnish Remover. They were pretty tough guys, and by their actions I considered them as being tough sailors.

Mud seemed to be everywhere on the base. A lot of it was brought in with our shoes. The mud was scraped off and shoved through the spaces between the boards, down to the ground below the building, which stood on posts. The floors then got swabbed with oil meant for heating the stove. In the barracks, the obnoxious odor lingered forever.

One washroom was available for every five shacks.

Sometimes, naked people were seen walking down the road with their toiletries. No female was ever in that vicinity.

Poor maintenance was evident all over the base. The unused areas were neglected, since horseracing was no longer active. Weeds grew along the track railing, utility shacks were abandoned, and mud puddles were in many, many places. In working order were the fire house, the water facilities, and the updated building for all of the Navy business. The chow hall was refitted with modern design and equipped to feed and move many troops in the very shortest period of time. Many had tight schedules.

Along the asphalt roadway, on the west side, facing the elliptical track, was the large roof of the grandstand over the large seating area. The peak was high – about 175 feet. A small enclosure, about five feet square, was built on that peak as a lookout point to observe fence-jumpers, fires, or any unusual activity. The entire base was visible from that height. A direct line of sight was available to report any incident as being unusual, mainly fires. A small, portable heater was inside.

To get to this cubby-hole-type lookout was quite a maneuver. First, we had to pull our body through a small opening in the roof, then crawl or walk on the roof to the peak – the highest point. My choice was to accept this duty instead of working in the galley. The next week I got stuck working in the galley anyway. For seven days, racking hot cups and bowls coming out of the boiling water of the fast-moving dishwasher, three times a day. It was not to my liking.

One could easily visualize horses running on the track just

by facing the circle on which they ran. Some guys jogged on it but found the terrain was so uneven that they stopped running.

A horse racetrack farther downstate also closed on account of the war's beginning, which was Bay Meadows.

Each day, the small Corsair fighter planes buzzed over Tanforan. Their practicing flight pattern was between the San Francisco airport and the Pacific Ocean. When coming in for a landing, which was the south end of the airport, they flew over the grandstand and the pilot's face could be recognized. The plane's propeller started revolving slower and the sound of the engines waned. Some pilots gliding in may have even cut off their engines. On one day when I was overseas, I heard one of the Corsair planes got caught in a downdraft and crashed into the grandstand.

In bed at night, the only sounds heard were plane engines of those landing or preparing to take off at the south end of the airport in the military section, which was only three miles from us as the crow flies. Many times our wake-up call was not sounded by the bugler but noise from the squad of planes preparing to take off at 4 a.m.

A few items of interest:

- ■ Tanforan is now a modern, popular shopping mall. Its location is in San Bruno, north of Route 80 and east of Route 82, twelve miles south of San Francisco – the same location as the horse racetrack and where the Japanese internees temporarily stayed, and finally the naval base.

45

- Suzanne Somers, a famous movie actress, was born in San Bruno in 1942
- Bill Hewlett and Dave Packard started their electronics business in an auto garage in San Bruno's neighboring city of Palo Alto. Locals already called it Silicon Valley and the area became popular very quickly
- In 2007, YouTube moved a few short miles from San Mateo to San Bruno.

The most appropriate area to drill and exercise was inside the cyclone fence on grounds adjacent to Highway 101, only 25 feet from the road, and the same spot where the vacated Japanese internees had their vegetable gardens. Some veggies were still growing there as we exercised. As traffic whizzed by, some pulled off the road to watch us. We always started with the sixty then 120 jumps per minute.

Our instructor was a Marine who participated in the invasion of Guam. He was 28 years old and appeared to be in excellent physical shape. He boldly demanded our full cooperation while instructing. We learned jujitsu and many offensive and defensive tactics. He pointed out to us more than once that the more you practice and learn the higher your chances of survival. A few smirked like they knew it all.

This led us to think that we were being trained to be commandos. Hip and bolo knives were already given to us to practice with. We practiced mock attacks on each other.

One guy drew a target circle on the inside wall of our shack. An officer was walking on the edge of the road, very close to our building, when the tip of a knife protruded through the building's wall with a bang. That upset him – too close for comfort, he must've thought. He opened the door and shouted to us, "No more of that, go practice somewhere else!"

Some needed more swimming practice, so our chief asked for those experienced to assist. Bud and I volunteered. We were then told that a bus would be waiting for us at the mess hall in the morning after roll call. I was surprised to see about twenty-five people fill the bus. Where did we go? Right to the YMCA in San Francisco. While the bus emptied, the driver said he would return in about four hours to take us back to the base. The desk clerk guided us to the pool's locker room After changing to our swim suits, we entered the pool area. We all were surprised with what we saw in the water: a ship's cargo net draped in deep water, its four corners tied to the edges of the pool. It could not be, but a second look gave me the message. Then Bud and I watched the sailors, who had a good time in the protective net. Soon the fun was over. We changed into clothes then headed back to Tanforan. I said to myself, Why did I forget my camera? What a picture that would've made, all caught in that net."

On the base each morning, the bugler drove in a Jeep with the roof open, standing up, one foot on the gas pedal, leaning over the windshield while sounding Reveille. He repeatedly played the tune, "You gotta get up, you gotta get up in the morning." It was loud and heard all over the base. Get-up time was 6 a.m. A few slept in a bit but were never late for breakfast.

One Sunday morning while making his rounds, in the

middle of his tune we heard a crash of the Jeep into the post which barricaded our building. The noise of the collision woke us, not the bugle. Everyone laughed as the bugle's sound waned down to nothing. He must have had fun the night before. He was not seen all that day. Probably hid somewhere.

We were hungry all the time. Our better friends were the cook and the guy who just received a package of goodies from home. They usually contained cookies, candy and cigarettes. The favorite drink was Coca-Cola. Those seven-ounce, green-tinted bottles were in the large, round vending machines located in many areas of the base. Some guys would rock the machine, upsetting the mechanism, which would pop a bottle out from the bottom without them paying for it.

There was another way I fed my innards with more vittles. At the first sound of the bugle, I dressed and ran quickly two bocks to the chow line at the mess hall for breakfast. When I got there, about fifty were already lined up. They must've had the same idea as me – eat, then return to the chow line again before the serving of food ended. I always thought the portions were too small.

Raising of the flag each morning took place in front of the grandstand at 8 a.m. Roll call was taken and then exercise – the jumping jack. A ten-minute break, then the assignments given to us for the day. Some duties did not fill the day, so then we were allowed to spend the remaining time attending to our personal needs. The important one was a haircut. If our hair was more than an inch-and-a-half long, no weekend liberty pass. The shore patrol at the gate checked each one's appearance and their ID before allowing them to exit the base. The barber was very busy on Fridays. It was time to ask my family to send me a pair of hair clippers. My dad had taught me to cut men's hair. Hair clippers were registered with the OPA, and only licensed barbers were able to purchase them. Somehow, my brother found a hardware store that sold him a pair for one dollar. After receiving them, I cut hair for twenty cents and saved some men from losing their weekend passes.

Even though we were assigned to specific barracks, we were allowed to meander around the base. I made friends and many cliques formed. We banged ears with the salty sailors to hear their battle stories.

The rumors began throughout the base that we would replace the CUB 1, 2 and 3 commando units, which had severe losses during an aggressive island landing. They were hardly spoken of. An office yeoman, a Navy clerk serving in the commander's office, picked up some bits and pieces of information and passed them on to us. At first it was rumored that we would be a LION 1, 2, and 3 group, but as it turned out, we became LION FOUR.

LION FOUR
U. S. NAVAL ADVANCE BASE PERSONNEL DEPOT
SAN BRUNO, CALIFORNIA

NB109/L81-6
Serial No. 397   27 November 1943

DECLASSIFIED

From: Commanding Officer.
To   :   The Chief of Naval Operations.
Via :   Director, Advance Base Office, Pacific.

Subject: Loading Plan.

1.   A loading plan for the overseas movement of
Lion Four has been completed and is ready for approval of the
cognizant bureaus.

2.   Lion Four loading plans have been drawn up
based on the following assumptions.

(a)   The destination is unknown. There are limited
facilities for unloading on arrival. There are no storage
warehouses and no docks as such, usable. There are no living accommodations for personnel.

(b)   Ships will be available to transport men and
materials approximately every three weeks and base equipment,
supplies and personnel will be transported in four echelons.

(c)   Echelons will be combat loaded and will proceed
direct to destination. There will be no staging of material or
personnel enroute.

(d)   Disembarkation and establishment of the base
will take place after the base site has been secured by combat
personnel, but base will be exposed to sporadic enemy attack.
Lion Four personnel are trained and prepared for limited combat
duties, but such duties should not interfere with the main objective
of establishing the base for service of fleet units without delay.

(e)   Construction Battalion personnel (P-1 units)
and Construction Battalion Stevedores (F-1 units) are available at
destination. If not, they will proceed the first echelon with part
of the Administrative (A-1), Communications Unit (C-1), and
Camp Units (N) for first echelon. C. B. personnel will set up camp
for first echelon, establish and construct the base and unload
the ships, assisted by Lion Four personnel. Lion Four personnel
will set up camp for succeeding echelons. Construction, repair,
unloading and transportation equipment, including trucks, cranes,

                        -1-   001129 104

When that was confirmed, it seemed to give us more of a
mind-picture of what would be expected of the group. It leaned
toward gunnery and ammunition services. Emphasis pointed to
learning about ammunition specifics: weights, sizes, markings, and

50

what damage occurs at their detonation. Almost everyone began to study for the next promotion, being a gunner's mate. I had to achieve the seaman's first class rate before working on that rank. Study manuals were very scarce. We shared them with worn pages. The pictures, illustrations, and reading material shown in them was such that a person with about a sixth- to eighth-grade education would be able to comprehend. To perform all the feats in the book would be a different matter. In boot camp, our commander told us if we were able to perform all the functions listed, we would be a ship's captain.

Three sailors: Stro, Arnie, and Lieutenant Thorne, all with gunner ratings, came from the east coast and joined our group. All three were first-class swimmers, deep-sea divers, and had just graduated the first certified class of underwater demolition (UDT). Their schooling taught them how to place explosives onto a vessel, object, or some property of the enemy while underwater for their destruction. Deep divers wore heavy helmets and shoes.

Chief Duncan asked if some of us would like to attend actual exercises and learn to set charges with them. About eight of us jumped at the chance. We formed together the next morning and after roll call took off on a bus. We headed right to a shallow part of the water in San Francisco Bay. There, the instructor exhibited his skill, setting charges and discharging them after swimming back to shore. I do remember that the fuse length was calculated by inches per second. A popular explosive was the Composition C. The color was light brown, soft, and as pliable as clay, and was easily attachable to many different surfaces. Our group did not use any explosives. Days later, everything went on hold on account of what occurred. Another instructor at Tanforan performed with a live explosive. With his poor judgment of the fuse length required, he did not get out of the water in time and was killed by the concussion. I remember the situation well, but was not there at the time.

At this period, I began to wonder why a group of torpedomen were grouped with us. They had trained in the Puget Sound in Washington. They used dummy warheads, not explosives, for practice. My friend, Paul, who was a member of the group, described to me how they worked on those greasy main engines and props. The gyros were cleaner and the more interesting job. Many of that group, including men with only seamen classifications, were also striking (studying) to become torpedomen. The two groups, gunners and torpedomen, intertwined smooth relationships throughout our stay in California.

Learning about guns and ammunition was still ahead for me. A shared book was all I had to study from. Listening to those with experience enlightened me about my future path. I knew it would be hard work. I weighed 148 pounds then, and to perform work of that sort, a minimum of 150 pounds was standard by the Navy. Seeing that some others accomplished this physically during some activities convinced me that I would be able to perform what was required to become a gunners mate.

Among our group, those being first-class seaman studied for the promotion of becoming a third-class petty officer as a gunners mate. To achieve that rank, one had to pass tests given by the gunnery officer. A six-month waiting period was required between each promotion, and only if there was a slot available. With the ongoing war there were many openings, therefore, some of the rules was adjusted.

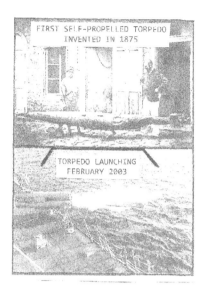

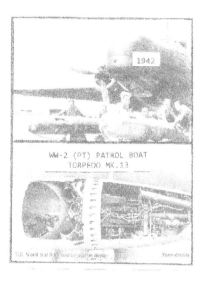

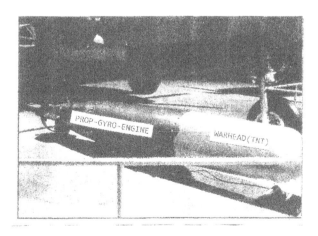

I was a second-class seaman and wished to follow that route, therefore that goal took two more steps.

Inside one building close by was the appearance of a conference room. It was the study room for all men on the base. If you could not find your buddy, he most likely was in that building studying, writing letters, or just getting away from the crowd. Many ranks of officers and enlisted personnel were seen with books open on the tables. At this juncture of my journey, I had some things to write about to my folks and friends way back home: the climate of the west coast, being able to see the snow caps on top of Mount Rainier, and how my daily routines were conducted while training. Of course, also how it felt living in a horse racing track without any horses.

One famous, cheaper beer was Rainier Beer. Those who would drink it called it the green beer, as it tasted bad. The better stuff, such as Bud or Schlitz, were shipped in from the east coast, but at a higher price. The underage, not able to purchase liquor, mingled with their elders and received plenty to drink. Our measly pay just covered the costs of visits to the surrounding cities. Some called home and begged for money to help out.

It was pointed out by some elders around the city area that it would be wise for us to tour and take advantage of visiting some of the more important sites available within our reach. If we paid for it out of our own pocket rather than having the military pick up the tab, it would be much more expensive, so we took advantage.

The Base Commander

The person in charge of the base in Tanforan was Commander Hopper. We all named him Hoppy. He was very strict, straightforward, and a starched-type officer. His style was always strictly business. HE looked about fifty years of age. His responsibility was to conduct all the events on base and also shape up the Lion Four group for overseas duty. No news was ever given to us about our next action or departure; only rumors. On occasion, he made surprise visits to our living quarters with short notice from his office staff. An inspection took place, with an officer assisting him, taking notes of anything that did not seem proper to him during his observation. He focused on each individual's bunk and the cleanliness of the barrack's interior. He did that famous "white glove" inspection. We knew that was coming so we did a good job dusting all the corners. We had two things in our favor: rough wood surfaces prevented him from wiping those areas, and the lingering odor from the floors swabbed with diesel fuel made his visits shorter. During our five months on base, we only failed inspection once. That was by not removing dust off the door tops at both ends of the building. Our weekend passes were allowed after rectifying the problem in his presence. Those in my barracks were quite neat in their lifestyle.

Every other evening and every other weekend were the standard schedule for liberties if no one had duties to perform or restrictions. Liberty was from 5 p.m. Friday until 8 a.m. Monday.

The lack of cash for most was the reason for remaining on base when liberty was available. Those having family nearby were permitted more frequent leaves as requested, if they had no duties to perform at that time. One buddy, Tom, had family in nearby Hayward, California.

Two shrewdies of the torpedo group had a way to get more than the normal share of weekend leaves. They were never caught. I never bothered to try asking or find out how they did it. They never missed or were late for the roll call in the morning.

First Weekend Liberty – San Francisco

At five o'clock on Friday, we went out the gate onto the waiting Greyhound bus. When loading, we all acted like a bunch of animals just released from their cage. Our first liberty off the base. Each of us paid the driver and off we went. The bus revved up and drove us on a twenty-five-minute ride straight to the bus station in San Francisco. The bus had terrible exhaust emissions from its overused diesel engine. New buses were not being manufactured while the war was on. The bus station was polluted with smoke. It was a relief to get off that bus and out into the fresh air.

We entered the main drag and parted in our selected directions. The hustle and bustle of the autos and people was no different than any other city. The two walking with me excitedly said right off, "Let's go get a tattoo." I paid little attention to them as I glared down the street and saw what appeared to be a military shopping center. Storekeepers knew that men in uniform would spend money. I skipped the tattoo and headed for the barber shop and entered it. As soon as I plopped down in the chair, a polisher started on my shoes. I did not need a shine – I wouldn't be able to leave the base if my shoes weren't shined. When I said no, he retreated with a sour-looking face. At the same time, the manicurist grabbed my hand to do her job. I loudly said, "Whoa, all I want is a haircut." With that remark, the barber did a quick job on my head.

How fast a sailor's wallet would be emptied, I then thought.

Again we got together on the street and noticed the cable car up on the hill. A decision was quickly made to ride it. We rode that rickety thing to the end of the line. There, the motorman got out and manually swung the car to the opposite direction on the turntable which had tracks built right into the surface of the street. When the car stopped, the passengers would get out and assist him. It was a novelty, and we also helped.

It was time to eat, so we headed for the café down the street. There we ate a bowl of chili, and while eating we all agreed to take in a movie. Not far away was the theater, which at that time was showing the popular movie, *Stormy Weather*. Lena Horne was the star and she sang the song named after the movie. We fell asleep.

The movie ended after midnight and we missed the last bus to Tanforan. The next available one would just get us back in time for roll call at 8 a.m. I felt like a lost sheep, needing help wherever it would be. It was a choice to either sleep in the theater or look somewhere else. We went out to the street and we walked and walked until we found a place around the corner from First Street with a sign hanging above the door that read, "50 cents per night." At our Navy pay, the cost of a hotel room was out of the question. We just needed a place to bunk. At the entrance we looked inside, and saw that it was a flophouse. It was a tough call. I looked inside and saw a few sailors who were really conked out. The other men in there were shabbily clothed and looked like they needed some salvation.

Because we were so exhausted, we decided to pay and enter. The old man at the door said to go in and pick a cot. A few empty ones were available. I searched and found one in the corner of the dimly lit room. The sleepers were snoring, sneezing, and blubbering. The cots had no pillows, my blanket was soiled, it smelled bad, and was worn. The floor had spatters of chewing tobacco, cigarette butts, and smashed paper cups strewn all over. I plopped on the cot and fell asleep in a few minutes.

Duty called at about 2 a.m. The plumbing in the small closet was not working too well, but who cared?

After an hour's sleep, something crawled under my shirt. It was a bug. I swished it away and it ran to join the rest of its friends on the floor. My eyes scanned down the aisle and saw the cots had their legs setting in paper cups. I got up to get cups from the holder on the wall to place under my cot legs, but the container was empty. I looked for help, but no one was around anywhere. I picked up four used, smashed cups off the floor and put my cot legs in to them as others had. I felt confident it would help keep bugs off of me. I could not sleep. The room was too warm and smelly. I leaned over the edge of my cot and watched those active critters on their playground below me. I could not believe this was a part of my life.

Time to get up. I slept in all my clothes and felt cruddy. We had to catch the bus at seven o'clock. It was only a few blocks to the bus station. We got on the bus and while riding, discussed better places to explore. It was a short trip back to Tanforan, and soon we were unloaded.

As I entered the barracks, some asked, "How was the weekend?"

My reply to them was, "Fine and dandy," with no further discussion.

The Pacific Ocean

While lying in our bunks, the discussion was about making a visit to the amusement park on the oceanfront. Bud and I decided to go on Sunday. The weather was as nice as anyone would want. We rode the bus to San Francisco and took another one directly west to the amusement area on the oceanfront. The carnival was in full swing. Military personnel were all over the place.

Our immediate focus was on the long building along the shoreline. It had three separate units under one roof. The first included bumper cars and a skating rink. The second had a freshwater swimming pool. The third had an open wall facing the ocean, which allowed saltwater to flow right into the shelter, making it an indoor sandy beach.

After enjoying some skating and riding the bumper cars, we entered the swimming area with the fresh water and had the place all to ourselves. It had a diving board for low-diving, and one for high-diving – a thirty-footer.

Bud said to me, "Did you ever dive from thirty feet high?" My answer was no. He then insisted I try it. He climbed up on the high board and made a clean dive that cut the water nicely. As he climbed out of the water, he said, "Now it's your turn."

I climbed up, and from the board looked down to the water below and became a bit leery. He hollered to me, "Do not look down, look with eyes straight ahead, then go for it." I ignored his statement, and becoming anxious, I dove and somersaulted, hitting my back to the water. IT stung and turned red for a while. I climbed back up immediately, did a quick dive as he first directed me, and he told me it was four-0 – 100%.

We swam for a while, dressed, then went to the amusement center for a snack. We only found a poor selection of food. It was apparent that the civilian front had problems with the shortage of food supplies, employment, and other bad situations confronting them. That caused many to make sacrifices. With of many, many items, our country's civilian population had to endure many hardships as the war continued, and things at home got worse by the day.

A Monday Morning at Muster

The gunners and torpedomen always attend roll call together in the morning. We saluted the flag, had the roll call, and did calisthenics. After being assigned our duties for the day, our chief gunner took out a newspaper from his back pocket. It was the San Francisco news. He waved it in the air, displaying the picture on the front page. It showed a tavern's smashed front window. Then he read a few lines describing that incident. All in our group remained very quiet. The chief raised his head, scanned his eyes over us, and said, "The police department in town would like to have names of any who were present during the fight that took place last night." He got no answers, but smirking came from the back of the crowd. He then dismissed us and as he walked away, a smirk was seen on his face.

Walking back to the barracks, two guys had scratches on their faces and one had a black eye – the two biggest guys in the group: Shulte and Tiger.

The story they told was that Tiger was insulted while drinking at the bar, a fight ensued, and the shore patrol was called in. They blocked the main exit of the tavern. Shulte and Tiger picked up a heavy game table and heaved it through the front window of the tavern, then escaped using the opening. They ran to a distant side street for safe haven.

One of the World War Two sayings was, "If no exit is available, you just make one."

Gun Training

One morning after roll call, as we were dismissed, Chief Duncan confronted me and asked if I would like to do gunnery training.

"Sure," I said. "Where at?"

"At Point Montara," he said, "and be ready with all of your bedding at the chow hall."

When I got there, about ten others showed up. The chief checked us off of his list as we entered the bus then he waved to the driver to go.

As we exited the base, we turned on a road westward, which entered the old Highway #1. We rode south on it for an hour and as the bus slowed. I saw a very small, inconspicuous sign on the ground beside the road. "Point Montara." The bus turned right there and we rode on that road for about five-hundred yards to the gate of the gunnery center. It was a naval base enclosed by a cyclone fence with security around it. We exited the bus, were checked closely, then were permitted to enter the base.

Ahead was our new home. A long, gray building with large windows. We struggled down the path to it with our sea bags. It would be the place we stayed for the duration of our training. It sort of looked like an institution.

Upon entering the building, we saw bunks bolted together, five high. The top one was near the ceiling.

After settling into our new accommodations, it felt quite comfortable. A nice cool breeze blew in from the ocean, the quarters were sanitary, and the meals were excellent; we were even allowed larger portions.

Our room accommodated about thirty. Most of the bunks were occupied. I picked one which was third-highest from the floor. When the top bunk was occupied, that person's body weight arched the entire column of bolted bunks toward the aisle. Looking out the window, not much was seen, only the fence surrounding the base and the prairies beyond, but neither guns nor any of the firing line were visible. The firing line from our building was about five-hundred yards away. Firing was directed by officers from a small tower behind the firing line. At the entrance was a large sign with red letters on it: "NO SMOKING." Many smoked during that generation. The famous brands of cigarettes were Lucky Strikes, Camels, Chesterfields, and Philip Morris.

The Routine on Base

Wake-up time was 6 a.m. The method used for waking us at this place was horrible. The song, *Sunrise Serenade* was played over the speakers inside of our barracks. It was only played for three minutes but seemed like an hour because the volume was at maximum. No one ever remained in their bunk to the end of that three-minute record. It even felt like my bunk rattled.

A lighthouse was located right on the coastline past the end of the firing line. Every five seconds, the light beamed through the windows of our sleeping quarters. The windows had no shades to cover them. When going to bed, we covered our heads with our blankets. The first night on base was very disturbing.

Firing times were announced over the base speakers with very little advance notice to report for practice. It was a hectic move if a bathroom urge came on. Day firing, night firing, and classroom instruction were pretty equally divided throughout our training.

The Firing Line

A whole line of guns were set in concrete pads on the high cliff facing the Pacific Ocean. We walked past all the artillery and viewed what was there.

The first gun in line was the .50-caliber (.50-cal), air-cooled machine gun. The next one was the water-cooled one of the same caliber. Then the 1.1-inch gun (Pom-pom). It was called that because of the sound it made. The next guns were the 20 millimeter (20mm), a single-barrel 40-millimeter (40mm), a quadruple 40mm on a trunnion, and the 5-3/8".

Those guns were the most widely used during the war in the Pacific Theater. Those who worked with and fired those guns were called "Small Gun Sailors." Guys who worked with the guns using projectiles up to 16-inch diameter were called "Big Gun Sailors."

My first lesson was on handling the small-caliber ammunition. This meant opening boxes, cartons, and many containers, some weighing up to 132 pounds. Larger cartridges were encased in containers designed to hold each one solidly in a fixed bracket.

My first try at firing a gun was the .50-cal air-cooled gun. It was belt-fed and fired over one-hundred rounds per minute. I had to grip it tightly when firing, and used short bursts in order to control it from swinging in all directions.

The next was the 20mm gun (Ack-Ack). It was named after

the sound it made while firing. The magazine holding the cartridges was filled and lifted onto the breech and locked into place. As a short person, I had to use a stepstool to lift that heavy load onto the breech.

When being the gunner of the 20mm, I had to fit myself into the shoulder straps, which were a fixed part of the gun. With the knee movements and body control of the weapon, it was time to set the sights on the target. The first time firing it was awesome.

The barrel became hot when firing it, and it turned to a fuzzy-red color. It was time to put on the canvas gloves to remove it and drop it in the pan of water to cool it. As it hit the water it sizzled, steamed, and floated for two seconds before sinking to the bottom.

When being the loader, my duty was to keep the deck clear of used cartridge casings as they fell out of the gun. They piled up quickly.

Once, while removing the casings, I got trapped beneath the gun, which began firing. Each shot vibrated my body relentlessly. I could not move while in the kneeling position until the firing stopped. I felt the muzzle's flashes hitting my face. When all was quiet, I turned and looked at the officers in the observation tower. Yep, one looked straight at me. No voice came over the speaker and soon the firing resumed.

It was important to understand each other's motions when guns fired, as no conversation was possible. Communication with the eyes was important. By that practice, operations moved effectively. Split-second decisions were made, and that avoided accidents. In practice, it showed those who had that quality in them, but those who did not required duty adjustments.

20 MILLIMETER ANTI-AIRCRAFT GUNS

40 MILIMETER (QUAD)
ANTI AIRCRAFT GUN

5"3/8 GUN

Among Naval historians, this dual purpose gun, for anti-aircraft and, other attacks was the best intermediate caliber gun of WW-2.

The 40mm Quad Gun

That gun had four barrels on a single mount, the trunnion. Each barrel was fed with a single clip holding four cartridges that were fed into the gun. The rate of fire averaged 120 rounds per minute. Its effective range was about 2,000 yards. It was a water-cooled gun and moved by hydraulic control.

On the day I fired that weapon, it happened to be a bright, sunny afternoon. About seven were on my crew. Much instruction was given to us in preparation for firing that gun. It was my first time.

The loaders were ready to load, the trainer checked the lateral movements, and I, the pointer, checked the vertical movements. Behind me stood the gun captain.

A rope was attached to a plane pulling a target red in color and the size of a wind sock used at small airports. The plane was flown by a civilian pilot.

The sun shined right in my eyes when the gun captain nudged me, signaling okay to fire. I fired at that long, round cloth as the plane was almost above our gun. I was told by the captain that I did okay, but I still wonder.

Night-Time Firing

Firing at night was different. More cautious movements were required when working in the dark. The possibility of accidents was greater. Each station was supplied with a durable Navy flashlight It lit up a good-sized area. That helped in finding the necessary tools and the handling of ammunition. Safety was of great concern.

Some of the ammunition we used was rejected by some who found them to be faulty during their use. They were either water-soaked, damaged, or came with a bad lot. Those at times caused jams, misfires, or explosions. Most came from ships after battles. Some were used and the rest were dumped.

One night in haste, I cut my hand while opening a sealed container of .50-cal cartridges. I bled quite profusely. I wrapped the cut with my hanky. When the round of firing ceased, it was taken care of.

A tracer shell was indicated by a white band painted around the projectile nose. A black-painted tip of a projectile was armor-piercing. Other colors painted on them defined their specific use.

In the dark, a tracer with a white band was used. About every tenth projectile placed in the gun was enough to see it light while riding through the sky on its trajectory. When firing many guns together, it lit up the sky quite brightly.

For two nights, an overcast sky cancelled the next forty-eight hours of gun-firing practice. During that time the foghorn blared "Ooo-aaa-ooo-aaa," for two days continuously. I looked out of the window and only saw fog. Something like being in the middle of the ocean. Many played cards or ping-pong. Lots of dozing, bull-crapping, and we just waited it out.

In the morning were class sessions teaching the 40mm. Our teacher was a second-class petty officer gunners mate. He served some duty at sea. With his second hitch in the Navy, I was sure some experience was in his background. His emphasis was on memorizing parts of the gun. Military equipment was designed to use the least amount of tools required for repairs.

A few men showed boredom in class. I absorbed his teaching with great attention. Class time was forty minutes.

One day at class, as the teacher began lecturing, he was called from class. As he left, he pointed to me and said, "You take over." That was a joke; why me? Probably by noticing that I paid attention in class. I tried to recite what was on the lesson sheet to no avail. It was a free-for-all until the time showed that the class period was over.

That same night, I studied the gun's parts and its uses. In the morning at class, no teacher. Everyone in the room just made noises. In the corner of the room, a couple of battle-worm sailors conversed with each other on the barrel springs recoil mechanisms of the gun we studied. I broke into their conversation and mentioned to them what I read in my book relating to the tension and compression of those parts. Then all ears suddenly perked up. Why? Because they began to relate actual stories of their experiences while at sea, pertaining to what we actually studied in class. Without any teacher, it was surprising how we began to learn from each other just by seriously listening to each other's opinions on the subject at hand. Our time in class seemed to slip by too quickly since we enjoyed the moods of all who were in the room.

For some reason, our teacher was never seen again, and that did puzzle me a bit.

I believe it was Thursday; a bright, sunny-but-cool morning. After the usual ceremonies – flag-raising, roll call, and exercising, my buddy Stove Pipe (we named him that because he smoked heavily) and I were assigned to clean gun parts encased in cosmoline – a gel-like substance that coated metal parts to prevent rusting. After unpacking, we placed them into a screen basket and cleaned them with steam. While doing that, the base speaker announced Stove Pipe should report to the gate. There he received an Army visitor from a military base in Salinas, California. After clearing security, they both came to our working area.

That staunch soldier, with a sharpshooter medal on his jacket, came right up to me and asked, "Do you know who I am?"

I looked for two seconds and then it registered. Mike, a grammar-school friend. He was twenty and I was eighteen.

During his boyhood, his main happiness was mostly hunting rabbits and squirrels along the banks of the Calumet River on the far south side of Chicago whenever he had money for BBs to shoot his gun. The majority of his jabbering on the streets almost always pertained to hunting.

While chatting, he explained to us his five-day leave did not allow him enough time to visit his home and family, therefore he chose us as his closest friends to visit It was his last leave before going overseas. I recall having the same predicament, and I was gone from home for twenty-seven months. We spent a happy time discussing our childhood, and the hour went quickly.

Mike had to leave us, and he showed his gratitude for a nice visit. While doing so, his face showed sadness. He then told us he was assigned to a large task force to be shipped to Europe in a few days. His position was to be in the first echelon of an invasion. It was not too long afterwards, just a few weeks, my friend Stove Pipe received notice from Mike's parents that their son was killed in action at the Normandy Beach invasion.

Am I In Trouble?

The next day before lunch, my name was loudly shouted over the speakers to report to the officer's observation tower located behind the firing line. That made me nervous. What did I do wrong?

As I approached the officer on duty, circled around him stood about eight sailors dressed in uniforms of a foreign country. The first thing asked of me was if I was able to understand the Russian language. I told him I did not. Then I was told why I was called.

Those standing near him were Russian sailors from their docked ship on the east coast. They entered our country's port as their safe haven. While in action with the Germans in the Atlantic Ocean, their ship's guns were destroyed. With inadequate artillery, it would not be possible for them to return to their homeland safely. Guns and ammunition were offered to them by us since they were our allies. They had to learn how to use our guns being installed on their ship. They were flown here for the training.

My Navy file showed that I spoke Lithuanian. Because both countries had some similarities in cultures, it might help to train with the Russian crew. It might also ease their tension.

From the beginning it was a sad affair, even though it showed that they accepted me as a friend. Their officer, who accompanied them, indicated to them in a very harsh voice that they work with great effort. We got along fine by using hand signals and funny words to each other. They worked very hard and learned quickly. I asked why they were in their dress uniforms and not in working clothes. Their answer was that when being on foreign soil, they had to be dressed in their best at all times. I felt sorry for them for two reasons. First, grease would be difficult to remove from their uniforms after training. Also, they were not allowed to mingle freely on base.

When they left, it was not a very cordial goodbye.

Another Weekend

Warner and I planned to visit Chinatown and the famous Fisherman's Wharf in San Francisco. Sunday seemed to be a good day, and we went. We walked through Chinatown and saw it being no different than the one that was in Chicago. Maybe more stores. Then we walked over to the bay and onto the wharf. The entire area smelled of fish and the sky was full of seagulls scavenging the waters for food.

It was a clear day and the island of Alcatraz was in sight. Around us was much talk about the escape of three prisoners just nights ago.

We walked the streets a lot that day. We took in an afternoon movie and then had supper in a nice eatery.

Time crept by faster than anticipated. It was late, about 11 p.m. The last bus to Point Montara was at midnight. In order to get a seat for that long ride back, we got on the bus early and took a seat in the rear, on the side to view the ocean. It was a good move.

Soon the bus filled with sailors, with the aisles filled. The driver was a lady about 28 years of age. She was as talkative as ever on the entire trip to our base. It was the old Highway #1 again. It ran along the coast on treacherous roadway. In many sections, the edge of the road was on a cliff overlooking the ocean. In many places it was rough and crooked. She barreled the Greyhound like nothing mattered. When she slowed to about ten miles per hour, it became scary. I knew what was next – a sharp curve which the bus was hardly able to get around. As the bus revved up out of the curve, I looked out of the window. With the moon giving me a clear view, I saw the rear wheels spin gravel over the edge of the cliff about fifty feet straight down. Most everyone was dozing at that time.

When we got back, some were still not balanced too well and had trouble climbing into their bunks. Those in the upper ones just pulled their bedding to the floor and slept in the aisle until morning.

One older gunner who acted as the father figure to us claimed he was only 35, but we knew better. More like fifty, He was slightly inebriated and had a problem climbing into his bunk. Then he looked at me and demanded I give him a haircut. It was 3 a.m.

"No way," I said to him. With that, he tried to punch me and missed. Realizing his action, he turned and went to bed.

He was a prisoner who volunteered through a program during the war that allowed those with minor sentences to complete their time in military service until the war's end.

A week at that place was boring. It had no recreation outside and only a ping-pong table inside. A vending machine hung on the wall with drinks and snacks. We were not even allowed to write home about our activities.

At the completion of our training, checks were handed out to us for the time we spent at Point Montara. On them was stamped for location: AT SEA. Not too far off, I'd say.

It was Friday night. The last practice went very well. Extra ammunition was spent. The sky appeared as quite a glamorous fireworks display when all the guns fired together. Nitrous fumes filled the air, but were soon blown away by the ocean's breeze. When all firing ceased, all the stations were put into their neat order for the next trainees to come on Monday. My station was at a 20mm gun pad.

It was about an hour before sack time, so some friends and I walked the firing line and looked at the guns resting after their untiring workout.

Ahead, we saw some celebrity in civilian clothing, busy chatting with our chief gunners mate. It was Cesar Romero who came to visit his uncle. He was a famous movie star who played in quite a few westerns and romantic movies at that time. The two spoke Spanish for a while and then Cesar, with his big smile, greeted us and wished us well on our journey.

Back at Tanforan

It was Monday morning and back we were. We settled in our barracks as before. Some new members were seen and were eventually added to our Lion Four group.

"Four-0." During my Navy time it meant 100%. If one buddy said "Four-0" to another, it meant 100%; okay. When firing a gun and the target was hit, it was Four-0 – 100%. If one answered all forty questions correctly on a test paper for promotion, it was Four-0. When one sailor wanted to relate "okay" to another when not verbally possible, he would signal with hand raised, touching two fingers together, forming a circle together to say Four-0. All is okay.

I wonder where it started? The forty questions on Navy test papers? Hmmm...

A new bunch of sailors entered our base. I wondered if they came to join our Lion Four group. After many rumors, they soon joined us and were smoothly nurtured into our spheres of activity.

My mind was on next week's liberty. My buddy Zook said to me, "Let's go to San Jose on the weekend."

That guy was always jolly and bragged about being from Yakima, Washington; the great apple-producing area.

I asked him, "What's so great about San Jose? I heard that place was deader than a door nail." In fact, the saying was that the mayor rolled up the streets and sidewalks and turned off the lights each night at 5 p.m.

When he mentioned that his aunt who lived there had a place where we could sleep and would make breakfast for us, that enticed me to join him on that visit. He also aroused my interest when he described some unusual sights to see around town. "You will like it," he said. Then I thought the trip would be worthwhile since nothing else was in my plans for that time.

On Friday evening we took off on a bus and rode it for 35 miles southward to get there. Even with that short ride, and because of being in the Pacific coastal region, it made a difference in temperature. It was a bit warmer than in the San Francisco area.

His aunt lived about five city blocks from the center of the business district. From the bus, we walked to her house and there she greeted us very gracefully as she came through the front door of her small, yellow, stucco-sided building where she lived. I asked her, "Where would we sleep?"

She answered, "Over there in the barn."

I went and looked inside through a small window and was surprised to see how neat and well-organized it was with two beds. My mind okayed it instantly. That night we rested well.

On Saturday morning she had breakfast ready for us, and while eating, she said to us, "You must meet my neighbor. He is a special person."

After eating, we went and knocked on his door and waited a short while. Then soon came out a very old man, who faced us with a bewildered look. Zook's aunt said, "I want you to meet a military veteran from the Spanish-American War." I shook his trembling

81

hand and he struggled to talk clearly as he gazed at the three of us. I cannot recall his name, and I doubt he was that old. This happened in October, 1943.

We decided to do some shopping in town. I, as most of the personnel did, had a picture taken in uniform at some photo studio to send home. Also a souvenir of some sort, identifying a favorite place visited while in California. Most people bought a colorful, embroidered pillowcase for Mom. On the satin surface of mine it had the lettering, "San Jose, California." It had three colors and was laced around the edge with silver shrouds. The store where I purchased it packaged it and mailed it for me. My mom responded with love.

There was no activity in town, so we decided to go and see a movie. We went to the oldest theater in the area. It was an old, wood-frame building. We paid and entered. The balcony was for us, so we began to climb up the narrow stairway. The walls began to shake. It lasted about fifteen seconds. Quiet for about thirty seconds, then a second shaking began that lasted a few seconds. It caused creaking noises through the building and dust filled the air. Some hollered, "It's an earthquake!" My hands were tightly gripped to the hand rail of the stairway and people jammed around me. Most ran out of the building so we had the choice of the best seats in the house. Everything seemed okay after the second quake, so we just relaxed and enjoyed the movie to the end.

Sunday was a good day to visit the city's Alum Rock park. We walked there, and up on a slight slope of the landscape was a large, round drinking fountain. It had five spigots to drink from.

Each had a different-tasting water. We just had to try all five.

#1 – pure, distilled water

#2 – the city's chlorinated water

#3 – very cold, deep-well spring water

#4 – egg-smell water

#5 – alum-tasting water

My least favorite water was the one with alum. It dried my mouth terribly. After doing some sightseeing, we returned to our base in the evening.

Ray, my buddy, whose hometown was Posen, Illinois, asked if I would care to explore a situation that he read about in the San Francisco newspaper. He suggested it might be worth seeing. It required a trip to the south side of the city at the Mission District.

With his brief description of what we might witness, it gave me a strong urge to pursue an unknown with him. "Let's go for it, became our agreement, and we went.

For a long period of time each year, only on Palm Sunday between nine and noon, swallows – "The Birds of Capistrano" – flew directly from the San Juan mission district of Orange County, California, right into crevices of the oldest buildings in the mission area south of San Francisco.

Our timing was perfect. While walking over there, past those buildings, Ray said to me, "Look up in the sky and watch for birds flying in from the south." Sure enough, we saw a few coming right toward us.

83

About five minutes later, a whole stream of them flew right over our heads and right into the ledges of the stone and wood structures on the street. Just like some magic trick, I thought. We also got bombarded with some spatters of their disposed excrement.

The weather was comfortable so we meandered down the street for some distance and admired the statues of the Blessed Virgin Mary painted in perfect shades of blue and white, sitting in the windows of most homes.

As we continued walking, many swallows began to fly away, and the remaining ones cooed loudly through quiet morning in the residential neighborhood.

All of the sudden, a huge bird swooped down toward our heads, as if attacking us. It really scared us. Its large wings flapped, sounding like two sheets of plyboard slapping together. It was a condor, probably checking on us. The condor is an almost extinct bird that lived in the southern part of California. That bird's beak was large and its body measured 45 inches long, having a wingspan of 120 inches.

More Duty Assignments

When we first entered Tanforan, we were told that all enlistees on the base would have to serve two weeks in the galley. Each would be contacted and told at some time. My turn came and I was assigned to work in the scullery. I was put on the job I dreaded most – racking cups, saucers, knives, forks, and other utensils used for eating. After they were washed in the boiling-hot water of the huge automatic dishwasher, I had to stack them in their proper places for the next meal. Even wearing heavy rubber gloves, my hands burned and stayed red until my duty ended.

On Monday morning, the chief came to me and asked if I cared to do my second week in the galley or go work in the fire department.

"Yes, fire department," I said before another word was spoken.

When assigned there, the first job given me was really exciting – washing fire hoses. There was a lot of work with the firemen. I had no fires while there, but the high weeds and building structures were of concern.

It was known that many petroleum fires happened on ships. Instructors formed small groups and taught us how to extinguish chemical and petroleum fires. Much of it was done by a wide spray of water or powder to blanket and smother a fire. We learned safety rules and life-saving procedures. We all had a chance to hold a hose nozzle and experience the extreme pressure of the water distributed from the pumps. I remember when it took two of us to aim a nozzle distributing almost one-hundred pounds of pressure. We practiced escapes from smoke-filled areas by using the hose for a lifeline. Gages were explained to us. It was emphasized to always remember the use of the buddy-system principles when working together. It was a very exciting week and made me feel stronger about tackling a fire in the future.

On the base each day, a group was formed to learn the use of a gas mask. We were told chemical warfare was possible since a war was going on. We practices by wearing a gas mask and entering a gas-filled building about the size of a two-car garage. While in there, we received instructions on how to cope with problems pertaining to gas encounters. After about three minutes, we removed our masks and exited the building. As I did this, I whiffed some gas, choked a bit, and my eyes burned. It was an awful thing to practice. Then the instructor told us an interesting and important story.

At one industry which manufactured gas masks, it was found that some faulty masks were leaving the plant. One employee who was either disgruntled or a saboteur punctured gas-mask hoses. The employee was an inspector at the factory, so all the masks passed his inspection by him.

It was found that he wore a ring on his finger that had a sharp, pointed tooth on it. His testing procedure required squeezing the hose to check for air leaks. Every so often, he tightened his grip on the hose and punctured it with that sharp, pointed prong of the ring. We were then instructed to always squeeze the hose to check for leaks before each and every use when we needed to wear the mask.

Now with three months of our stay at the base and no mention of shipping out, we wondered what, when and where our next training would be.

Transfers continued and new members joined our group every so often. Those in charge of the Lion Four group were a lieutenant, warrant gunnery officer, chief gunners mate, and a chief torpedoman. They arranged all of our training schedules and personnel moves with the approval of the base commander.

We were treated well by them. Most of our free periods were used to study for our next promotion. One person in our barracks was a magician and displayed his talent to entertain us. The time seemed to slip by fast. Some played cards, some washed clothes, others ironed their uniforms, and some of us just laid around and bragged about our cultures and home life. About three practiced jitterbug dancing. The ones from the south had words that left their mouths with a twang. When the Brooklynites spoke, they could not lie about where they came from. The farmers and fishermen had some wild tales that seemed to never end.

Bold Men of the Seas
Merchant Marines of World War Two

The organization consisted of men and ships that carried supplies across the ocean to the fighting zones. They were not a part of the Unites States Navy, but they worked and served with them as a team. They lost 733 ships and 8,652 men of the 215,000 who served.

The ships had a minimal amount of armament to defend themselves because they almost always were in a convoy escorted by the United States Navy.

For some reason, those men never did get the credit or recognition they deserved for what they accomplished as a part of the fighting team during World War Two.

The United States Merchant Marine refers to either United States civilian mariners or to a fleet of US civilian and federally owner merchant vessels. Fleets were managed by either the government or the private sector.

Their fleet of ships played the most important role during World War Two. They traveled all over the world and carried cargo of all types, including fuel, ammunition, planes, tanks, vehicles, and other items necessary for fighting the enemy.

Many ships were sunk by German U-boats while crossing the oceans before and during the war. Some went down as close as the Gulf of Mexico and the shores of Florida and Virginia. Many were sunk by the enemy when our code was hacked and our ships' routings became known to them.

When our men were not yet notified to serve in the military, some signed up with the Merchant Marines. The pay was about the same as our military.

"THE UGLY DUCKLINGS." "WORK HORSES OF THE DEEP"

It took only 50 days to build one, 2,710 were produced. When loaded to their safe levels, on deck, extra cargo was added. One ship loaded was able to carry,-- 2,840 Jeeps, Or-525 Armored cars, Or-525 Ambulances, Or-260 medium sized Armored Tanks, Or-525 2 1/2 Ton Trucks, Or-156,000 boxes of Rifle Ammunition, Or-217,000 crates of 75MM Gun Shells.

By rail, to carry this amount required about a Mile and a Quarter of freight cars.

Many ships were in demand. They were mass-produced and called Liberty Ships. Many of the crews and captains of those ships came from foreign countries and assisted in the military movements in the Atlantic and Pacific Oceans.

To join, men first had to pass the physical examination. If they passed, they could sign up to serve. The next step was to observe what two ships were listed on the billboard on the office wall. Crews were needed to serve on them. The ships were loaded with either fuel, ammunition, or other various cargo for the needs of our troops to fight the enemy. A member was able to choose either the first or second one listed on the board. If no choice was made, he would then serve on the next ship listed, regardless of what the ship was loaded with.

Some skipped when learning of the ship's explosive content, and would miss boarding the vessel on its departure. They would be considered AWOL and were hunted, and if found would have to bear punishment.

I believe the Chicago area recruiting station was on Commercial Avenue in South Chicago. I can only remember one of my acquaintances who joined that service, but he skipped and was never found or heard from to this day, according to his brother.

When possible, our navy protected or escorted those vessels on their voyages. The total ships in the United States Navy lost during World War Two by percentage was 0.88%. Losses in the Merchant Marines were 3.90%.

Originally, the officer candidate school was run by the Coast Guard, but later the United States Navy took over.

Rust showed on the ships very soon after coming into contact with saltwater. Continuous maintenance was required to keep them in ship-shape. Those mariners were always seen tending to their duties on board. At times, when the ship would list at fifteen degrees while on the rough seas, the work continued, even up high on the masts.

The Merchant Marine World War Two Veteran status was denied to them by the so-called Civilian Review Board run by the Air Force. It was finally granted Veteran Benefits status in January, 1988, for only those who served during World War Two between December 7th, 1941 and August 15th, 1945.

At A Merchant Marine Base

On a November morning, after breakfast and roll call, before the group dispersed, Chief Duncan loudly asked if anyone cared to go to a Merchant Marine facility to practice some of their training exercises.

I was there next to Bud, my swim partner, and he said to me, "Let's go."

I quickly answered him, "No, it's probably a competition event."

He approached the chief and inquired what was expected to take place over there. The answer was that the entire place was for our use only and no one else would be there. That changed my mind. We inquired what had to be brought with us, and we were told to bring only swim trunks and a towel; some sandwiches would be provided at lunch time. That sounded okay to me, so we ran to our barracks, picked up our stuff, and got back to the chow hall just as the bus came to the gate for us. The sky was overcast and it was cold outside, about 57 degrees. Many said it was too cold and did not go. Only about ten got on the bus.

We rode for about an hour and across the Bay to a cove that had very still water in that particular training facility's area. It looked like a commando course above water. On the site was a large barn filled with an assortment of ship-type apparatuses.

Our first order was to go inside the building, change into our swim trunks, then pick a life vest off the wall and get ready to start an exercise.

Our gunnery officer who came with our group was our instructor. He ordered us to attach the vest straps tightly around the chest and legs. Then he said that when jumping, cross the legs and cross the arms below the chin to avoid a head-snap when hitting the water.

The wooden structure to practice on was a wide, slanted platform with a 45-degree angle all the way up to thirty feet high. It had open spaces between each slat and water was seen below through each opening.

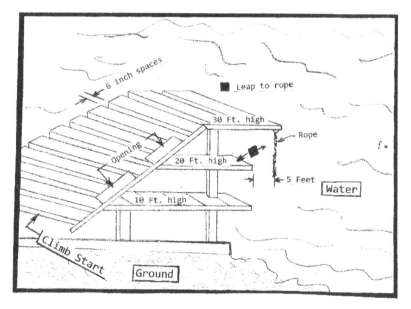

As cold and as squirmy as we were, we lined up to start. We began, one by one, to climb the angled platform – some hesitantly – to the ten-foot-high jump area. There, we took turns jumping in the water. Bud was first to get out of the water, hollering that the water was warmer than the air.

After we all took our turns jumping, we had a short break. Next was the climb to the twenty-foot platform and jump. Some were hesitant because jumping into the water from that height was never done by them.

One in our group, Warner, was quite fearful, but said to me, "I have to do it because I want to know how it feels like, if and when the time comes when it would be absolutely necessary for me to jump for my survival."

The last exercise was the toughest. We had to get on the twenty-foot-high platform, and leap off the edge out to the rope dangling from above. It required a jump of five feet horizontally through the air above the water to grasp it. If not enough momentum was attained by lack of thrust, or we lost grip of the rope, one would drop and make a nice splash in the water. Many laughs sounded when someone was not successful in that exercise. A few were able to slide down the rope to the lower platform.

After practicing, I asked if I could make a dive from the top platform.

Gunner said, "Can you do it?"

"Yes."

He said, "Go."

I prepared to do good by making a nice dive snice I saw many watching. I got up there, looked straight ahead out over the water and made a perfect swan dive. A little cheer was heard.

94

All the practice ended and we all were anxious to get dressed to leave and get back to Tanforan. The bus did not have a heater so we shivered all the way back. It was so nice to get back and we all hugged that glowing salamander oil stove in the barracks. It was also close to the evening chow, which we looked forward to, being very hungry from those exhilarating exercises. In the evening, many in the barracks had questions.

The following morning, after most had their duties assigned to them, my chief pulled me aside and ordered me to go work in a shack located on the far north side of the base. I walked to that building and saw how messy it was, outside and inside. I entered and saw a sailor working with a stovepipe on a work bench. I had seen him often on base and now I had met him. He was a second-class boatswain, serving his second hitch in the Navy. He was a deep-sea diver, and one of the four on base who just recently completed a course with the group in the first Navy-certified scuba-diving schools, which was on the east coast.

He looked up at me and asked, "Can you weld?" I told him I could not. After a short, quiet, spell, he said, "I will be right back."

He was gone for over half an hour and I thought he forgot about me. He finally returned carrying a 100-pound bomb casing on his shoulder. Most were manufactured containing explosives, but the one he had was empty. It was about six inches around and thirty inches long; a good size to be a carry-on tank.

Fighter pilots used the empties, filled them with water, and attached them to a nosecone filled with colored powder. They dropped them down to a target floating in the water to practice aerial bombing. When the colored powder smashed on the water, it showed them if it was a hit or a miss.

A small oxygen tank, about 24 inches long with a little apparatus tied to it, was what divers had in mind. Normally, a heavy body suit, steel helmet, and lead shoes for diving was the only unit used, and it was a hassle.

On the bench, we removed the four fins from the end of the bomb casing. He asked me if I was in the Navy V-6 program. When I told him I was and had a job waiting for me at war's end, all was quiet. He glanced at his wristwatch, saw that it was 4 p.m., then said I could go back to my barracks.

In his eyes, I saw how intent and serious he was with the project he worked on; something new. Little did we know how scuba tanks later would be so important in industry and entertainment all over the world.

I assumed he picked up a new helper for his project who had a Navy career in mind. That may have been the reason I was not called back.

We Are Navy Connected

What took place in 2015 was a surprise to me. I, with my wife, and my friend Steven and his wife, one day went to the Mabenka restaurant. We went to that one particularly because it serves Lithuanian-style food. It is on 79th and Cicero in Chicago.

Steve is a Korean War veteran. When we go out together, we make it a point to wear the cap having the military insignia on it. Sometimes it gets us a discount.

When we entered and were being seated, I slowly removed my jacket. Then, from two tables away, a man in his fifties hollered to me, "Hey, Navy! I know what Lion Four is!" He obviously saw the insignia on my cap.

I walked over to his table where three other people sat with him. All shook my hand in recognition for my military service, and I thanked them. Then he told me he was a Navy veteran. I asked him if it was okay to talk after we ate and he said it was okay. We ate, then I visited his table.

I asked him, "How is it that you know about the Lion Four group?"

He explained to me that while he served, he was a deep-sea diver. During their instructions at class, they also discussed the history and progress of diving, which included the scuba tank's development. He said he heard of the instructor who was killed in underwater demolition practice while demonstrating to his class in October, 1943, at Tanforan. I told him it was a shallow-water event and that I was there.

We both soon became quite comfortable in our conversation, most of it the situations we experienced in military life. I noticed a pair of crutches beneath the table where he sat. I asked him, "What happened? Why the crutches?"

With a voice softly starting out like it was coming from a

distance, he told me of the mishap. He was medically discharged from the Navy as a result of getting the bends from his last experimental dive. He said to me, "It was too deep."

It left him with a loss of muscle strength in his body, and tiny air pockets remain beneath his skin, making him uncomfortable.

Time passed quickly with ears listening to the short and long tales we told at the table. It was finally time for him to depart with his company, and he stopped and told me he was an American Legion Commander of a post in the area. I cannot recall which one.

There are other situations that occurred along the way in my life similar to this one, all of which connected me to my past in the Navy.

A Civilian Labor Shortage

Some who were bunking with us in the same barracks had their home close to base and visited their families more frequently. A request had to be granted by their immediate officer for an extra visit. When they returned from visiting, they always had news for discussion. It pertained mostly to first, which neighbors entered military service and those who were serving, then about food and their needed living supplies which they were short of.

Tommy, my friend, had family living in Alameda, which was just across the San Francisco Bay. He always had the latest news. He once spoke of the two places that paid top dollar for employment. One place needed a handler of highly volatile chemicals and nitroglycerin. The other one was cleaning the remains of whatever was left in the holds of damaged vessels returning from the battle zones. I am sure it was a gruesome job.

Military pay was not too great, so some tried all kinds of jobs. Those who were married and had families to support couldn't cut the mustard, so to speak. It was rumored that a few tried those higher-paying jobs but did not last more than a day.

Some employers took a chance and hired some handicapped men and women, and the underaged.

A Bad Weekend

During the last part of February, the weather became warmer in the San Bruno area. We became anxious to spend a weekend off-base. Paul and I agreed to visit San Jose, and we prepared.

My uniform was ironed, shoes shined, and I got a haircut. On Saturday morning, we went out the gate to the bus stop across the highway. There, on the shoulder of the road, six or seven vehicles were parked, offering sailors free rides to those going south. A very good deal, we thought, so Paul, another sailor, and I jumped into the back seat of an auto which contained two middle-aged ladies. We expressed our appreciation for offering us the free ride. That had been done quite frequently in that area for servicemen.

The lady took off like a hot-rod driver. While driving, she began swinging her head back and forth as she talked to us in the back seat. That was not good, I thought, because the auto kept drifting on and off the road at a pretty good clip. The odor of alcohol from those women permeated the air inside the vehicle.

They asked, "How far are you going?"

We looked at each other in the back seat, and quickly Paul answered, "Only to San Mateo," which was the next city. He lied. San Mateo was another thirty miles.

The lady passenger said, There is nothing going on there."

Paul replied, "I have to visit a close relative there."

She pulled off the road, slammed on the brakes, we got out and she took off like a racecar driver leaving in a cloud of dust. We walked to a bus stop, got on a bus, and completed our journey.

In town, I decided to reserve a room at the St. Claire hotel for the night. It was a bit expensive, but for that one time, what the heck? As I was signing in at the desk, it happened to be the last room available for the night. A Naval officer standing behind me begged me to give him the room. I told him I needed to sleep just as much as he. Some time later, I thought that if I was ever assigned to serve under his command somewhere – uh-oh.

Paul and I separated from the other sailor. The two of us enjoyed the entire day as we explored pretty near everything while walking. We took in a movie then it was sack time. Paul had a place to stay, so before heading back to the hotel, we agreed to meet at a restaurant the next morning for brunch.

At the hotel desk, I requested a 7 a.m. wake-up call. In the morning, I woke, dressed, and walked around the corner of the hotel to the St. Guadalupe church and attended services. When the offering basket came around, I reached for my wallet and found that it was not on my body. I became frantic. I ran out of church to the hotel, ran up the steps and into the room that I slept in. Two maids were inside, cleaning the room. I ran over to the bed where I slept, reached under the pillow where I put my wallet, and I found it. I was quite relieved. I had over fifty dollars in it. By inflation evaluation would that be like five-hundred dollars now?

Late in February, a new member entered the base and soon was fitted into our Lion Four group. He was out of boot camp for only about three weeks. He was eighteen and about my size, a bit over five feet tall. We became acquainted in no time at all. He was friendly, and his name was George.

He asked if we could walk around the entire base one evening, even if it took an hour. We did, and as we talked, I brought him up to date on our past activities and exercises we performed. We returned to our barracks and sat on a bench outside. At about 7 p.m., a yeoman came from the commander's office and looked for George. He found him right beside me. George was handed an envelope which had a telegram in it. It read that his brother was killed in action.

After he read it, he raised his arms up and started to scream, "Oh no, oh no, it cannot be." Then he began to cry so loud that it attracted those in the next barracks, and they came over to see what went on.

When he calmed a bit, I asked him, "Where did your brother serve?"

He answered, "In the Army in Europe, and it was my third brother. They all fought and they are all dead now. Now I am the only one left with my mother."

Later, he told me that his mother tried to talk him out of

enlisting in the service, but he felt it was his duty. Then he faced me with a sad look and said, "I cannot figure out how I will be able to still face my mother when I see her."

A short while later, a Jeep pulled up to our barracks with two shore patrolmen who found George and told him to pack up and go home.

While packing, he kept repeating to me, "I don't know what to do now, I don't know what to do now."

His discharge papers had on it, "Family Hardship." A situation of that sort was usually channeled through the military with the chaplain and the Red Cross.

After all of that, it was getting dark, with the sun setting over the horizon in the west, and a few of us began to tell each other about which members of our families were in the service. None had more than two. I had one serving in Europe with General Patton's Army.

It took me a while to fall asleep that night, as I kept thinking of George and what was ahead for him.

Visiting A Pecan Farm

I was reminded more than once when mingling with civilian elders while on the west coast to explore and visit all you can; it might be your only chance and it may cost you later.

While at Zook's aunt's house, she invited us to visit and see a pecan ranch. It was owned by a couple of her friends in Salinas. She saved enough of her gas ration coupons for the trip. We knew about her vehicle that was about to take us there. It was a 1932 Model A Ford Club Coupe. She had a box built on the back to make it a small pickup truck. I believe that began the trend for the popular El Camino and Ranchero pickup trucks that had some popularity between 1960 and 1975, manufactured by GM and Ford.

We left early on Sunday. She drove with Zook sitting beside her and Paul and I on the wood floor in back, behind the cab with a blanket over our legs to shield from the wind.

The six cylinders sputtered smoothly during the entire ninety-mile round trip. All we saw on both sides of Highway 101 was barren land as we sat and gazed, while smelling a bit of the pollution from the vehicle's engine.

We finally arrived there and met the couple who owned and worked that small plantation. They gave us a short tour as we walked around the pecan trees. That night it was predicted to have frost in the air, so they covered the trees to protect them from damage, and also had a number of smudge pots that burned oil to help keep the temperature up in the entire growth area.

The main problem they encountered was that when World War Two started, an employment shortage began and they had to struggle with less help during the harvest period. They had three sons and all three were in military service. One was on a base close to home so he was able to contribute some of his time when it was direly needed. When a serious problem occurred in that area, the Co-op system by the neighbors got together to alleviate any problem that existed.

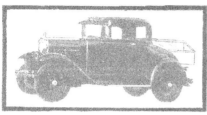

In the box is what we rode in to Salinas and back for the 90 mile round trip.

The rumble seat was removed. A box replaced it. It was started by the Chicanos on farms in the San Joaquin valley.

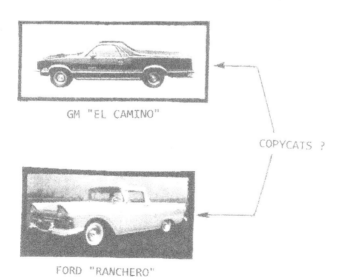

GM "EL CAMINO"

COPYCATS ?

FORD "RANCHERO"

We talked a lot, mostly about their sons that were serving overseas and what the three of us sailors were going through at the base and so forth.

The time moved quickly and we had to depart from those nice folks. We got in that vehicle, with Paul and I in the back. We sat down on that short wooden vehicle bed and covered our legs with the blanket, and were quite chilled on the entire return trip to San Jose.

We had faith in that vehicle to get us back, but there were concerns as we listened to the sputters of that engine all the way back, moving at 60 mph.

A Seasoned Sailor and Survivor

It was February and the weather showed signs of shredding the frosty days in San Bruno. Every day, the sun shined brightly through the windows of our barracks. With the clear skies, it was a great advantage for the pilots with their small Corsair planes to practice their flying. Their route was always the same, from the south point of the city's airfield, over our base, to the ocean and back. Most of their practice was done early, about 6 a.m., and also 2 p.m. At times the buzzing back and forth sounded like buzzing bees, A droning sound was also heard from the larger airplanes at the field, which seemed to be only a stone's throw from our base at Tanforan. At noon, the noise always subsided. We knew the reason for that of course; it was lunchtime.

At about 2 p.m. on a Sunday afternoon, as we quietly lay in our bunks, all of the sudden the door opens and shuts with a loud bang. In came a tall, lanky, unshaven sailor who walked across the floor noisily and asked, "Where is there an empty bunk?"

We pointed to one and on it he plopped down his carry-on bag; he had no sea bag. In the bag were some wrinkled clothes, his shoes were not shined and he did need a shave. He appeared to me as a person who never had to apologize to anyone or for anything of any circumstance.

Believe it or not, he had one green eye and one gray eye. He saw that we were slightly appalled at his appearance. We did cater a bit to his sludgy behavior by laughing with him as he told a few raw jokes. He was a second-class boatswain serving his second hitch in the Navy. He looked a bit salty to me.

He sat down on a bunk and in a loud voice said, "Now I have a new home." He scouted through his small bag and pulled out three straight razors, with a sharpening strap that he used for shaving. He unfolded one razor held it up in the air and said, "I keep my razors so sharp that they could split a hair in two." As I looked at what he was doing, I began to wonder if he had a problem of some sort because of his unpleasant behavior. He rattled on about this and that, and then showed us that he actually could, and did, split a hair in two with one of his razors.

He began pulling one article of clothing out after another from his bag and laid them out on his bunk. Each item was stenciled with a different name or number but none belonged to him. We immediately questioned him on that point.

His answer was, "I lost everything I had when my ship, the USS Yorktown, which I was on, sunk during the Battle of Midway on June 7th, 1942."

The following are pictures of the USS Yorktown (CV-5) – at dock, under fire, rigged to another ship, putting out a fire, at sea, and finally capsized in the sea at Midway.

109

When he made that statement, his eyes widened. Then he said, "I went on leave, and when I returned, everything new was supplied to me, all new garments and a sea bag, but it got lost on my trip over here. I saved these here in my ditty bag with the different names on them from what shipmates gave to me when I was rescued. The clothes I wore got soaked in oil when all of that happened. I decided to keep these, the donated ones, for a while."

As he began to tell us about the battle and other incidents of his career in the Navy, he said, "It's a different world out there." After listening to him, I felt that I was still wet behind the ears as a sailor. What annoyed him the most was that he was being shuffled from place to place too often.

On his last day with us, he said, "I would like to show you guys something that I learned." He left and returned with a parachute. He was gone for some time, and where he got it from I did not know.

We made space on the floor and he opened up the chute that stretched from wall to wall in the barracks. He described the proper folding procedure to us while answering our questions. It was made of silk, the chute and shrouds. As the war progressed, silk was unavailable and a substitute material replaced it. Each fold he made had an explanation to it. His last statement to us was, "Remember, if you need to use a parachute, and if you can, fold your own."

The Survival Seminar

Before going overseas, we were all required to attend a seminar that told us how to prepare and what to expect when arriving and entering enemy territory. It began with the movie, *Kill or Be Killed*. The theme of is was, "If one does not psyche himself to kill, then he might be injured or killed." That gave us all a scare and then everyone in attendance really paid attention to the movie.

After the movie, the next item was about survival of the fittest. Preparation was the key word on the subject. Keep equipment clean, in good working order, and be sure it is ready for use at a moment's notice.

Last but not least was the subject of hygiene. In the tropics it was horrible. One must cleanse as often as possible. One must maintain body health for one's self and others. At some times, a difficult period may be like when an uncontrollable biological urge comes upon you and you will suffer. In that case you would have to dispense while fully clothed and at some time later take care of that not-so-pleasant situation.

In the tropics of the Pacific region, for those who needed to get close to or land on an island, they would take a pill called Atabrine, which helped resist malaria. It would be taken three days before entering any mosquito-infested water or land. A pharmacist would administer the pill and no one would leave the ship until the pill was consumed. The pill was yellow, the size of an aspirin, and very bitter.

When I left the building where the seminar was held, my head spun with all the new information just presented to me. From that day on, my actions became better, and with a more cautious and serious attitude. I felt like, "Hye, I am getting older."

Back at the barracks, we practiced more with maneuvers using our hip knives. It was noted to us that the Japanese did not have the ability to do boxing as much as men did in our country, so that would be a good fighting advantage.

In the next few days, rumors from the office help came around again. It was about a departure schedule and what to expect while crossing the ocean. The talks floated like they had some merit that came from our officers and it would be just a week or two before our departure. It was mentioned that we would land on an island and to be rifle-ready when landing ashore.

At that point, we had the opportunity to check out a rifle from the base armory and we practices with one, challenging each other. The standard .30-cal. Rifle had the bayonet, which when detached was also used as a hand weapon. However, the carbine; the sniper rifle, did not, so the hip knife would then be used.

That evening, we discussed a lot about the seminar we attended that morning.

Overseas Preparation

Strong rumors spread all over the base that the time was near for our departure. Then, one officer in command came in and told us that all the leaves and liberties would be cancelled soon. We were told to be prepared to leave within the next few days. The waiting period stretched out to about ten days.

Some of us talked about how our beneficiaries would spend the money if we did not return from overseas. Some women had married quickly, for love or not, so as to not lose out on a good thing. The insurance payment was ten grand.

A base officer came into our barracks and invited us to a going-away party on Friday evening at a San Francisco hotel dining room to be given by the USO people. It was for our Lion Four group only, so that was a positive clue that our departure was near. About thirty of us attended.

Upon entering the dining room at the hotel, a boutonniere was pinned onto our jerseys by an elderly lady who was in charge of the affair. The place was filled with females of all ages. A couple of musicians played music and we were all asked to dance. There was a table in the corner with some strawberry punch.

Two sailors knew the punch would not be spiked, so they brought a small bottle of liquor with them. One of those two was seen at times being able to do a chug-a-lug with a whole quart of beer until the bottle was empty.

Well, that night, that guy had a half-pint of whiskey on him. He pulled it out from beneath his jersey and bragged that he could drink it all without stopping. Well, he sure did, but then he turned away from the small bar that was there, he looked at us and fell flat on his face to the floor and passed out. The shore patrol was called in off the street and they hauled him away. When he saw us days later on the base, he did not care to talk about that evening. Everyone was nice that evening. We all chatted, danced, and some exchanged addresses with each other. The party broke up about midnight. After a nice evening we got on a bus and rode back to base.

On base, everything got locked up. It was bad for the few who lived close to the base and no longer could visit home. The few phones on base were always busy with lines formed at the booths forever.

During those last few days, officers meandered around the base and noticed that so many all of the sudden wrote letters. Our chief came into our barracks and reminded us that in our letters not to even hint of our departure, only that we still had no information of our next move. Then, at the same time, he mentioned that those testing for higher ranks could try for them. That is when I, with a few other second-class seamen, took the test. We all passed and were promoted to the rating of seaman first class.

Departure

On March 27th, 1944, about 5 p.m., just as we were going to chow down, our chief came into our barracks and hollered, "Okay guys, this is it, be ready in an hour to leave." Heavens no, pack and unpack again? Not this time. It was for real. The buses pulled up to the base for us to get onto. Some made jokes to cover up their nervousness. I think many of us did. We packed quickly and when we got on the bus, the barracks were emptied in no time at all.

With the buses loaded, we rode quite fast through San Francisco and over to a pier in the Oakland shipping area of the ocean. At the dock was this 500-foot-long, gray-colored ship with *USS Seaflasher* painted on its bow. We got off the bus and threw our sea bags onto a cargo net, which was lifted onto the ship then lowered into one of the bottom holds. We kept our ditty bag with us. It contained only one change of underwear, soap, and a toothbrush.

That is when Bud said to me, "That's all you need. We are going where it's warm." We lived out of that bag for the entire trip. Then it occurred to me that I had twenty-three cents in my pocket and I showed it to Bud. He said to me, "There won't be any place to spend it, so why don't you just wait until we are out in the ocean and throw it in the water for good luck?" I did.

We formed a line and walked up to the deck of the ship, where we each were checked off of the name list by our chief. From that moment, we acquired a new boss. He was a second-class gunners mate and his name was Mack. He led us down below decks where bunks were assigned to us. Mine was on the port side, up against the bulkhead, so close that when lying in it, if I turned my head to the left, my head would touch the cold steel of the ship.

The bunks were made of canvas held by a steel frame and only thirty inches wide. The only light came in from the entrance, and at night was a dim red light that lit the lower section of the ship. That area smelled like dirty old rags, even with the fans blowing all the time.

After a short rest, we climbed up to topside for instructions from Mack. He said to form groups of about ten or so, and choose buddies if desired. He specified an area where each group would hang out for the entire voyage and reminded us to be there when needed. Then we were told that we would act as armed guards for the entire voyage. Since we had enough men in the gunners group, our watch hours would be four hours on and twelve off. My lookout station was in the 20mm gun tub on the starboard side, amidships section of the second deck. When scanning the waters, each had to overlap their marginal viewing areas to cover the entire periphery of the vessel when on watch duty.

It was time to look over our new home. We walked and settled at the fantail. Food scraps were piled up there. To prevent scattering by the wind, the pile was blanketed with a canvas sheet until dark to be dumped overboard. Dumping during daylight was not a good idea because the litter would be more visible on the water and would leave a trail for the enemy to see and follow.

It was eight o'clock and no dinner. Some picked food scraps from the pile and ate them. Mack saw that and said, "Stop it, chow is ready now."

A line formed and we went below and ate. With our stomachs filled, we returned to our hangout by the railing and enjoyed the cool breeze. A few who had girlfriends and wives back home all of the sudden cried like babies.

A worrisome expression was seen on many of us as we had to face the unknown, which would be soon. *What will happen next?* I asked myself.

USS SEA FLASHER

On watch, we were to report any object, moving or not, on the water or in the sky. The main objective was to watch for vessels on water or aircraft in the sky and report them immediately. We studied the aircraft and ships of ours and the enemy's with photo cards. We challenged each other to see who recognized them the fastest.

It was almost sundown when a tugboat approached the ship. A dock hand came out from the pier building and unhooked the bow and stern lines from the bits. The lines were pulled up by the merchant seamen on board and placed in their proper place on deck. The tug slowly nudged the bow of the ship away from the dock, turned it around 180 degrees, and faced it toward the ocean. The props began churning in slow-motion and a minute later the acceleration was increased as we approached the Golden Gate Bridge. We were all in awe as we looked up while passing beneath it. The skipper had the ship's bell ring and the horn blared loudly as the stern passed the bridge. Then we were out to sea.

We all sang a short song, *Goodbye America*, as we headed west into the sun going down over the horizon. I looked back and watched the cars on the bridge get smaller and smaller until they were out of sight. Then the engines revved up to eighteen knots per hour, its maximum speed. Nothing but water was seen in every direction. As the waves got larger, we heard them splashing against the hull.

After two days out on the ocean and talking about how beautiful the blue water was, we then talked about being outside the three-mile continental limits of the United States. The limit is twelve now. Then one guy pops up, "We are pirates of the open sea; no more restrictions." We all laughed.

At about 4 p.m. on that sunny afternoon, the general alarm sounded and the speakers blared, "Now hear this, now hear this. Man your battle stations. I ran up to mine as others did. All was calm, only the waves were heard splashing. After about twenty minutes it was announced, "Now hear this. All clear."

We returned to our hangout stations. That event was never

explained to us. The rumor was that we entered one of our submarine's travel paths. That made us wonder why having just one hundred or so onboard the ship made us ride so low in the water. Later we found out that tons of bombs were stowed in the holds below the deck.

In many cases, captains of ships were given orders not to be announced to the passengers. That definitely was our situation. He might have had the travel and destination information, but it was not known to us. I never saw the captain. All the orders given to us were from our Lion Four officers and petty officers in charge of our daily movements. Mack was our boss and he only gave us orders, which was usually with short notice.

A Sailor's Initiation at Sea

It had been seven days since we left California. Our location was right on the equator, east of the Gilbert Islands. It was the first time on our ship, the *USS Sea Flasher*, and most of the sailors on board were crossing the equator for the first time. I looked for a meridian line but couldn't see it – ha, ha.

We who had never crossed the line were called "Pollywags." Those who had crossed the line at any previous time were called "Shellbacks." Those who had some experience were asked to assist those who conducted the initiation ceremony, which put us pollywags through a fearful situation that would make us feel more manly. A mixture of all ranks participated in this event.

King Neptune (a boatswains mate) was Master and Director of the court. He wore a paper-bag hat and a small mustache made of manila-line strands. A few shellbacks assisted him.

Davy Jones (a signalman) was Neptune's chief courtier and dressed in a black pirate suit.

Neptune's wife (a carpenter's mate) was a mophead and wore a hula skirt.

Serafini, the royal baby, (the chief radioman) wore a diaper made from a mattress cover.

The Royal Judge (the ship's chief engineering officer) was dressed in black.

The Royal Devil (the ship's cook) was dressed like a pirate more than ever.

The barber and the dentist in their garb were ready to do their job. The shellbacks were ready to start as the stage was set.

CROSSING THE LINE

KING NEPTUNE

DAVY JONES

NEPTUNE'S WIFE

ROYAL JUDGE

SERASINI

ROYAL DENTIST

ROYAL BARBER

SHELLBACKS

ROYAL DEVIL

POLLYWAGS

SOMEONE SAID IT WAS FUN

DAVY JONES LOCKER

The ceremony began after the morning muster, about 9 a.m. We all were told to report topside. The weather was overcast and the temperature was comfortable. We sailed smoothly over the waves.

We pollywags were told to strip naked. The shellbacks attacked us with water from a fire hose. Then we were prodded with a low-voltage unit which was called *The Devil's Fork*. Then we were led to the stage to listen to how unworthy we were. We had to hear the fanciful charges against us, and had to be willing to accept the challenges ahead of us.

When we agreed to those terms, it started with the dentist doing a mouthwash with some vinegar, paprika, or diesel fuel. The barber cut our hair as he liked and shampooed it with machine oil.

Running the gauntlet was the worst. I had to crawl through a thirty-inch diameter tube, fifteen feet long, naked. I was scrubbed on the behind with a coarse brush and prodded as I exited it to face a fire hose, then splashed with food scraps. The finale was being paddled with wooden slats, and not too gently by one shellback standing on each side of me.

After all was done, we showered and one by one we crawled up the throne's steps and faced King Neptune, who certified us as shellbacks.

I have to mention what a blessing it was to have a rain shower after that ceremony. The ship's shower used salt water, and it did not mix well with soap; it gelled on the body. Only the Fels-Naphtha brand worked slightly better; it did not gel quite as badly.

We enjoyed the rest of the day conversing on how we endured the initiation. Some older salts joined our conversation and bragged about how they passed their initiations. At his initiation, one said, he was blindfolded and pushed off of a gangplank, not knowing that a cargo net was there to catch him before he fell into the ocean. That would've been scary.

Below the equator, the ship zig-zagged a lot for protective measure from the enemy submarines that were on the prowl. The ocean's breeze was no longer cool, but hot. Our travel became more easterly. We constantly focused on the horizon.

At a distance, a cloud formation simulated an island. Bets were made to guess which was which. Those with sharper eyes won the bet.

My station on the ship was near the bow, and therefore I was able to see where we were headed all the time.

On April 11, 1944, we entered the quiet harbor of Noumea, New Caledonia. Our ship anchored close enough to view activities at the beach area. A few were transferred from our ship for re-assignment. A certain amount of our group requested to go ashore and were permitted. When I stood at the railing, I saw nothing of interest so I stayed aboard.

A couple who returned brought news that one sailor from a ship previously in the harbor went ashore for a swim. He ventured in slightly deeper water than he should have, was attacked by a barracuda and drowned.

After three days, we pulled anchor and headed straight for Milne Bay in New Guinea. It was a few days' journey. In that area it became very hot. We were told to keep our shirts on to protect us from the extremely hot rays of the sun. We also had to keep one arm through the life vest as we entered an unsecured fighting zone.

When the ship's pharmacist handed out the Atabrine pill, he mentioned that the Anopheles – the female species only – carried the fluid that caused malaria. We laughed. How does someone protect one's self with that information? By getting the pill, we knew that land was near. It was a good guess; we saw land the next day and we headed right for it.

As we neared the harbor, we saw the huge U-shaped hill that surrounded the cove. It was a deep-water harbor, so our ship anchored close to land.

Milne Bay, New Guinea

New Guinea is one of the most malaria-ridden areas of the world, despite many preventative campaigns. Twenty-three to twenty-nine percent of the fighting personnel were incapacitated from that cause alone. It caused many delays in fighting the enemy. Because of its dense jungle growth and rough terrain, it hid some enemy fighters, and they somehow survived until the war's end. The average temperature for the year in that region is 115 degrees.

The fighting in the bay region ended in June, 1942. Buna, farther up, was cleared in December, 1943, and Finschafen was mostly cleared of enemy fighters by February, 1944.

We saw a lot of activity in the harbor area. Boats were running back and forth, ships signaling each other, and the noise of the equipment loading cargo onto the vessels going to the fighting front. The harbor was very busy.

Noises echoed from the jungle, and occasionally some rifle shots. We anchored in murky water and it was very still, like a lagoon. Mosquitoes surrounded us like we were to be their main meal. The pungent odor of some jungle rot was a bit annoying. There was no breeze at all. There was no shade. IT was over 100 degrees and perspiration just poured from our bodies.

Our group's station was in the sun all day long. We could not touch the steel anywhere around us without getting burned. We removed our life vests and shirts just before we entered the harbor. It was two o'clock in the afternoon. The ship's anchor was solidly gripped by the mud so the ship did not budge a single bit. The bow was the highest section of the ship raised out of the water. We had to remain at our station, which was close by.

Bud said to me, "Let's jump in for a swim." Without me answering him, he threw the climb-back-up rope over the side into the water and jumped in, clothes and all. He looked up at us who watched and yelled to me, "Kapo, come on in; the water's fine." I saw him hanging on the anchor chain. I looked to see if any officers would see where he was. It looked okay to me so I jumped in next to him. We hung on the chain and enjoyed the refreshing water.

We soaked for about five minutes and then looked up to see if any officers saw us. We did not dare to move away from the ship for fear of being seen. It felt so good and we said all the guys should be in the water with us. We invited them to join but they just nodded a *no* sign.

Bud said, "Let's not stay too long, some water creature might find us and we would be in trouble." We looked around and then decided to climb the rope back up to the deck. It was a struggle for Bud but he got up over the railing.

Then I climbed and became exhausted about six feet from the railing. I decided to wrap the rope around my ankle to rest my body. It helped, but it left a rope burn on my skin. Finally, with helping hands, I got up and over the railing.

The water felt so good. We left our dungarees on our bodies

to dry and put our shoes on because the steel of the deck was so very hot.

About twenty minutes passed then the speakers came on and hollered out, "Now hear this. Anyone jumping ship will be thrown in the brig immediately."

We all looked at each other and remained silent. We wondered, *how in the heck did those officers find out?* Maybe they saw us.

During the next few hours, some read stories from their little pocket books – Agatha Christie was one – and the others just waited for chow time.

At about 9:30 the sun disappeared under the horizon, then the ship's lights turned on. A garbage scow, pushed by a small boat, came to take the food scraps from our ship. IT tied up right beneath our station's railing where we always hung out. All we had to do was jump over the railing and we would land right on the pile of food scraps. This was a valid clue that we would be pulling anchor within the next twelve hours. A light came on and focused on the barge for the work crew to remove our garbage. Our ship was the last to be unloaded in the harbor.

A snake slithered out of the water. It looked around and then it slithered onto the scow and over to the food scraps for a meal. Its body was about ten inches thick, and it was about twenty-five to thirty feet long by our guess. It definitely was an anaconda. It nibbled scraps of food from the pile for a few minutes, then its head turned around and slid back into the deep, murky water in seconds. Then that became our lengthy conversation.

It was late, but natives down the line were jabbering and singing as they loaded vessels with cargo going to the troops. It was an interesting sight, and occasional, ongoing noises from other areas were heard all night.

The jungle rot smelled and the mosquitoes buzzed around us constantly. It was too warm to sleep below decks. It was midnight when another head popped out of the water in the exact spot where the snake did earlier. It was the head of a huge turtle. With its large claws, it gripped the edge of the barge and climbed up far enough to get some of the food scraps. Its neck and claws were about a foot thick. The body was about six feet long, four feet wide, and two feet thick. Right at that moment, a spotlight from the upper deck focused on it. Then the speakers came on.

"Now hear this. Anyone wishing to swim may do so, but only on the port, bow side." This had to be aimed at Bud and me again. We all laughed a lot and I was sure the officers on the upper decks heard us.

The rainfall in that area was about 200 inches per year. When seeing all of that thick, wild, wild growth of the jungle area, it sure appeared to be the perfect environment for the larger, rugged creatures of the wild.

The short airstrips were constantly covered with water. Even with blanketed, perforated steel sheets, it was still difficult for aircraft to land and take off, which was required frequently.

At night, signaling between ship and shore was less

frequent. Even though the commotion would subside, some activity around the docks would continue.

At about 1 a.m. the air was not so warm so we went below decks to sleep. It was about 6 a.m. when I had a nightmare. I dreamed that the same snake I saw on the garbage scow scavenging scraps earlier in the evening was in my bunk, wrapped around my body. I suddenly awoke, shaking, with my heart beating rapidly, then I realized it was only a dream. I stood up next to the bunk and felt the ship moving.

I put on my life vest and ran up to topside. Many were already at the railing so I joined them. Our ship was moving smoothly over the small waves. The sky and the water were as blue as ever in every direction. We were on the move again.

I went down to the galley and ate. Then I returned to my station and joined the rest of the group to face the next unknown stop.

We sailed for three days and wound up in Buna. That beach area had all flat land. As we moved toward the beach, I saw the ship moving too fast for the shore. The captain ordered to drop anchor at his chosen location. The ship kept moving.

Over the speakers, the captain hollered, "Drop a couple more shackles."

It was the first time his voice was heard on the journey.

The engines were already shut down and the ship was drifting toward the beach pretty fast. Then he hollered very loudly, "Drop all the shackles." When that order was enacted, the anchor chain slid through its housing so fast that the grease on it smoked like it would catch fire. It sounded like thunder.

Most of the chain ran out and a slack in it occurred. Then it was waiting time, to see if it took hold. It was an anxious period. In about fifteen seconds it did. I watched the anchor chain as that happened, and saw those three-inch-thick links become elongated. Then our 500-foot long, 7,000 -ton ship, the Sea Flasher, swung around the anchor very slowly and we wound up very close to the beach.

When the anchor was pulled up to leave, the props stirred up a lot of mud, which showed we were in some shallow water.

We moved northward along the coast for a day and wound up in Lae.

When in Lae, very little was told of our next move. We stayed there for one day then moved out, and wound up in Finschafen the next day.

The fighting there had been over for just two months. Planes flew out to the east and into the fighting zone in the Great Britain Straits. Our ship was not a fighting ship so we just stayed back and waited for orders to move on. But we stayed there for only one day.

IT was a beautiful day when we pulled out into the Bismarck Sea. The waves were small, but when we got about fifteen miles from the harbor, they became large and smooth. They were called swells, and it felt like sliding over Jell-O. When sailing over them, one moment the ship went twenty feet high, and the next moment down twenty feet, just like riding a roller coaster. A second guard rail was put up as an extra precaution. As the ship sailed over each swell, it plunged profoundly with a long, angular sway down, then back up to the next swell. During that, we all felt like we were at the mercy of the sea. When the ship was on the crest of a swell, that city-block-long vessel's stern was seen in the air above the water. The props chattered and that part of the vessel vibrate. As we stood at the rail, we could almost reach the nearly vertical wall of water with our hands. There was no splashing of water, just a smooth surface all over. As we scrounged around the deck, one of the merchant marines came over and explained to us that when two storms ended, some underwater movement let them meet each other and caused those huge ground swells.

At night, we strapped ourselves in our bunks. Absolutely no activity was seen for those two days and one night as we braced ourselves somehow most of the time.

When I laid in my bunk, Ray said to me, "Look at the welded joint of the two steel plates of the bulkhead right next to your head."

I turned my head and looked. What I saw was seepage of water coming through the hull of the ship. At once we said, "It's a Liberty ship." A welder on the production line in the factory who worked on our ship must've had a bad morning.

I kept my eye on that leak but it did not worsen for the rest of our journey.

Eventually, the swells decreased to a point where there were no more waves as we entered the Bougainville Channel, the entry to the deep-water Mariana Channel, which is 6½ miles deep.

It was about 2 a.m.. The water was still as ever and quiet. The engines stopped running. I was on the second deck in a gun tub standing watch. The surface of the water was as smooth as glass. It seemed like the lull before a storm. There was no moonlight and it was scary.

Mack gripped onto whatever he could and fumbled his way to each of us. He said an engine needed some repairs. To me it seemed a bit far-fetched, since the ship was brand new. Then he said nothing could be thrown over the sides, not even spit. One smarty did spit and when it hit the water, it sounded loud and formed a huge, expanding ring on the smooth surface. AN officer soon got to him and gave him a stern warning he would not forget.

That alone told me something might be lurking nearby.

When I heard the engines start a half-hour later, my nerves were relieved. We moved very slowly until the moon lit up the water. That allowed us to move faster.

The next day was very hot as we headed for the equator. In the warm water, we saw many flying fish. They were about 12 to 20 inches long. They propelled themselves up to 24 inches above the water. They were able to fly about 150 feet before dropping down into the water. They were also able to attain speeds of 40 mph. We clocked one that flew in the air for 55 seconds.

There are about 65 species and they date back to over 65 million years ago.

ack came over to us and said we would not be served chow for a few days. The cook said the food supply shrank because our travel orders were altered and extended. Instead, we were given K-rations. The ration was in a small, wax-sealed box about 3 x 6 x 1½ inches in size. It contained a small can of salty, ground meat called spam, some crackers, cheese, a bouillon cube for soup, and a hard chocolate candy bar. There was a similar ration in the same sized box with different foods in it called the C-ration.

Most of our troops were familiar with both kinds, and rations were distributed when it became necessary. Many mocked them, but when no other food was available, they cherished them as close as one would watch his wallet.

Ray, Pete, and I went right to the tip of the bow, leaned up against the bulkhead, and watched the waves splash beneath the hull as we sailed over them. The up-and-down movements felt like being on a see-saw.

At forty-five degrees to our right, we saw a large gray whale heading right toward us. It skimmed the hull of the ship as it passed right beneath and kept on going. A smaller one followed and passed behind our ship. They both continued on as though nothing even mattered. It was the first time I ever saw whales.

On the 26th, in mid-afternoon, an officer shouted loudly over the speakers, "All hands take cover below decks. Gun crews report to your stations."

I was not on duty, so I, with all the others, quickly scrambled for cover to the closest hold of the ship, which was the amidships area. Too many ran down in that hold and we were squeezed. An attack was expected. With insufficient air movement down there, being at the equator and so hot, it was horrible; a few passed out. They could not fall down because we were all so tightly packed together. I felt a bit woozy myself. Water just poured off of our bodies like a wet cloth going through a wringer. My attention was on the ceiling above me, and I waited for something to happen. A minute felt like an hour. My friends standing nearby looked at me pitifully with fear. Those moments were so silent that one would hear a feather if it bounced on deck.

We heard a plane zooming overhead. A minute later we heard it again and then it was quiet for two minutes. "All clear" was heard over the speakers. I was relieved of my tensions as were others, I was sure.

We hurriedly ran topside and saw the plane that flew over us, and it tipped its wings and flew away. It was one of our planes, the *Wildcat* (F4F). Then we were told our destination was Manus Island and we would be there the next day. We had no idea what we would see when arriving there.

The Admiralty Island Invasion – Code Name "Brewer"

I t was time to form a new advance base to continue forwarding supplies to our fighting forces. General MacArthur accelerated his timetable for capturing more islands. He ordered aircraft to make some immediate reconnaissance. They flew north from New Guinea and saw a group of islands.

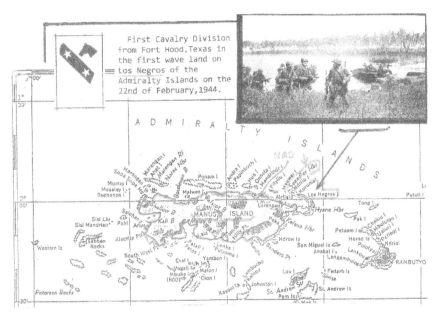

First Cavalry Division from Fort Hood, Texas in the first wave land on Los Negros of the Admiralty Islands on the 22nd of February, 1944.

The Admiralty Islands, which lie 200 miles northeast of the New Guinea mainland and 300 miles west of Rabual, are only two degrees below the equator. The climate is tropical with constant high temperatures and high humidity. Rain there is a constant thing. December to May is monsoon season, with winds coming in from the northwest.

The largest island is Manus, sixty miles long and 19 miles wide. Los Negros is right next to it but only connected by a crude wooden walkway over the small ravine next to it. Pitylou Island is across the water, a few miles to the east.

Manus is very mountainous, with peaks as high as 3,000 feet and all covered with thick, tropical rainforest. It was an uncharted coastline, having numerous reefs and consisting of mangrove swamps all over. With each heavy rain, the water runs downhill so hard that red clay mixes with it, and it would wind up in the ocean as a large Y-figure with small red swirls forming that shape.

USS Phoenix (CL-46)

Admiral Kinkaid with General Mac Arthur
Outside the harbor before the battle.

On February 28, 1944, General MacArthur and Vice Admiral Kincaid were on the *USS Phoenix* (CL-46), a light cruiser which left New Guinea and came to the Admiralty Islands to support the invasion of Los Negros and Manus Islands. A close scrutiny of the islands was made by the air force. Photos and information were gathered together, then a small group of men were sent to an isolated beach area to see what was there.

Upon entering the jungle area, they surprisingly found that

it was occupied by Japanese soldiers and well-fortified. Some large gun installations and many machine-gun stations were ready for use. With all the facts collected, the Americans prepared an attack and invasion of the islands of Los Negros and Manus very soon. The code name became "Brewer" on February 26, 1944.

It was determined that those islands had to be taken with an attack in five days. To do that, high-speed transports (APDs) were required as beach landing crafts – the LSTs and LCTs were too slow. The difference in speed was eight knots per hour.

Only three transports were available: The *USS Brooks*, *USS Humphreys*, and *USS Sands*. Each accommodated 170 men. The 1,026 men were carried by nine destroyers: The *USS Bush*, *USS Drayton*, *USS Mahan*, *USS Reid*, *USS Stevenson*, *USS Stockton*, and the *USS Wells*.

The Admiralty Islands

The islands were discovered by Schoten and LeMaire in 1616, four years before the pilgrims landed at Plymouth Rock. They were colonized by the Germans and were kept until the first World War. Then the Bismarck Archipelago and the northeastern part of New Guinea were given to Australia to administer under mandate by the League of Nations.

The Japanese invaded the islands in April, 1942, and were held by them until February, 1944, when they were bombed, invaded, and taken over by the United States military, and declared secure in May, 1944.

Casualties of the Admiralty Islands
Japanese dead -3,820; prisoners – 75
American dead – 360; wounded – 1,189; missing – 4

The islands are spread over a sea area of roughly one-hundred miles in diameter, the largest island being Manus. Next in size is Rambutyo, which is east of the group. Los Negros, a hook-shaped island, is attached to Manus Island, practically surrounding Seeadler Harbor.

Seeadler was the name of the ship that first entered the bay. It was raided by Count Von Luckener and was made into a useable base.

Other harbors are Hyene, named after the survey vessel, and Alacrity Harbor, taking its name from the British government.

Manus Island's commodities are coconuts, copra, and bananas. It has the notoriety of having a great variety of birds, the most beautiful seen anywhere.

With all things in place, General MacArthur and Vice Admiral Kinkaid stood on the bridge of the *USS Phoenix* (CL-46) outside the harbor as they bombed Los Negros Island. Then the fighting task force under the command of Rear Admiral Fletcher landed his invasion forces with the First Cavalry Division, led by General Smith, on February 22nd and wiped out the Japanese by the 28th.

Manus Island was invaded next, and on the 17th and 18th of March, the important Lorengau Beach and the hill above were taken. A small garrison of Japanese were wiped out at Lugos Mission. Then, basic needs were set up at Lorengau Beach. Sporadic firing continued to be heard for days back in the jungle. Security by soldiers and observation by aircraft continued for weeks.

It was time for us to get onto Manus Island. Our ship's signalman repeatedly asked for someone to answer his request to lead us into Seeadler Harbor. It had been cleared of mines and our sonar buoys were in place. A message came back to our ship's signalman that an escort would arrive. Two island natives in a small boat came to our ship. One jumped aboard and ran right up to the helm cabin. The native was familiar with the waters in that area, and he guided our ship into the harbor. As we slowly entered, I watched our boatswain take readings with his fathom line. It then became obvious to me how valuable the native's knowledge of the waters was by seeing the ship's hull skim within inches of the jagged corals.

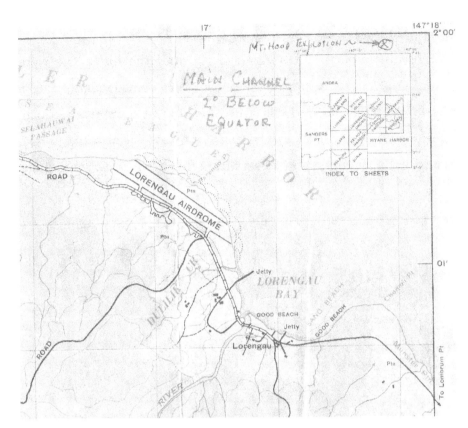

We finally anchored in Seeadler Harbor, Manus Island, on April 28, 1944 and we stayed on board overnight, then we waited for orders to embark. Next morning, that was it – we packed and lined up to leave the ship. A cargo net was slung over the side for us to climb down to get into a landing craft waiting in the water below. We threw our sea bags in. Then we were given our rifles and we all climbed in as well. After loading, it was a short five-minute ride to the beach. Our sea bags piled up on the sand and I found mine without any trouble. On the beach there was a lot of commotion that lasted about an hour. Mack came to us, handed out K-rations, and told us we would sleep on the beach. My first problem was thirst. A 500-gallon water tank on wheels came. The

144

water tasted bad because the inside of the tank was coated with tar.

The strange surroundings with messes all over from bombings left land crabs, centipedes, and even koala bears looking for new hiding shelters.

We each were given a raincoat which actually was half of a pup tent. Two halves formed a tent but one person occupied it while the other was on watch duty. They all had a design of camouflage colors and were made with a rubberized material which made them too warm to wear.

At about 8 pm a gasoline generator was set up for lighting and an assortment of tools were laid out in piles, including 24-inch-long shovels to dig a foxhole. We were told to pick a partner to share a pup tent, but when using it, the other person would be on watch. Darn it – my partner became Wiggy. He was a nervous person. He talked me into digging a foxhole farther up on the hill. We dug a small hole just big enough for two to sit in. With three swats of my machete I chopped coconut trees that laid on the ground and placed them around the hole we dug to form a wall. When dried for about five days they became hard. So far, with the invasion completed, I began to think, "What am I doing here?"

Mack came to us and mentioned that some of us would be transferred and the rest would work with ammunition by serving fleets in the harbor.

Two nights sleeping on the ground was too much. On the third morning as I awoke, the skin on my neck was eaten away by some insect that left a wide, raw, red surface. I bathed my neck carefully and in two days it was much better.

We received tents and were told to take them anywhere up and over the hill from the beach. Ray, Sims, Pete and I chose to share one, and staked it to the ground in a short time. Each tent was given a flashlight. We kept our rifles and a canteen of water with us at all times. Cans of mosquito spray (DDT) were abundant. Nets supplied to us to cover out cots blocked some air. That tempted us to fold back the netting, which made it feel much better.

Ray was the first picked for the night watch. He walked the perimeter of our camp of about seven tents. The first night, at about 11 pm, Sims woke and shouted out loud, "Look at this, you guys!" Awakened by his shouting, I saw him focus the flashlight on a mosquito drawing blood from his forearm. It had legs three inches long and with a beak just as long. With its beak filled, it appeared to resemble a thermometer.

This was not the end of Sims' attacks. At about six in the morning, he hollered out, "I'm bit, I'm bit, I'm done for!" A centipede, seven inches long and a half-inch thick, with its arched back, had its two needle-like prongs stuck about a half-inch into its belly. He quickly knocked it away and smashed it. We found our group's pharmacist. He looked at the bug and told Sims it was not poisonous. Then we kidded him about bringing his companions with him from his home state of Alabama.

The next night was my midnight watch. I patrolled the far end of our camp's perimeter facing north. The weeds were over knee-high. I was fully clothed, patees on for leg protection, long-sleeve shirt with my sleeves rolled down and a steel helmet on my head. It was a bright, moonlit night. Then I remembered what Ray told me that day. "It's scary out there; keep your eyes and ears open every minute. You will hear many strange sounds but don't be trigger happy."

As I started my patrol, my first thoughts were of my own protection. I moved my helmet strap from around my neck and placed it tightly on my chin so as not to be strangled. I removed my ID tags tied on a wire around my neck and put them in my pocket for the same reason.

Large birds, which we called "midnight canaries," flew back and forth above the trees across the jungle, screeching so loud with their eerie sound that continued all night. Huge bats, clearly seen with their large, flapping wings, were seen scooping up mosquitos from the jungle growth and the eucalyptus trees.

I registered my mind to anticipate an enemy attack. If someone approached, we were taught to ask, "Who goes there?" If they had difficulty in answering, then we asked some question like, "Who pitched the last game for the White Sox last year?" It would be very obvious from a wrong answer or fumbling speech. Then a decision would be made to kill or be killed. "Hi, Joe" was their famous trick.

One story was told to us about how tricky the Japanese were. When fighting in the jungle, and seeing it was hopeless, they would release for surrender a female companion some had in their camps, naked to our troops. When approached, she would raise her arms and two hand grenades dropped from the pits of her arms that would kill her and those near to her. We also were told to look for those hiding, strapped and hidden in the trees.

The only incident that occurred on my watch was a grunting noise close by. Then a nibble on my leg. It was a wild boar pig, so I swatted it away with the butt of my rifle. Firing my rifle would identify my position to a possible enemy. We heard shots every so often in the jungle all night long by those searching for an enemy, and not too far from where I was patrolling.

My friend Barny had his rifle taken away and was given a different duty because he fired his weapon during his night watch and could not explain the reason for it. He was labeled trigger-happy and was considered dangerous.

One morning, I followed Paul and Barney on an exploring adventure. We were told not to go far from camp. Well, we went over a mile away where a crude sign on a post was marked, "Booby trap area." There was a vacated native shack which had been used as an office by the Japanese. I followed those two right inside. I saw shrunken heads on the wall, obvious in the native cultural practice. I took some pictures with my small bullet camera but lost them. Paul collected the Japanese items for souvenirs. He eventually donated them to the Lion Four exhibit at the Nimitz Museum in Fredericksburg, Texas.

A small Quonset building was put together by the Seabees for a chow hall. Some fresh food arrived from Australia, and yes, it was mutton. What else, with their famous sheep grazing in that country? The line of men waiting to eat was as long as ever. I held guard duty with my rifle outside as the line moved slowly into the building. A last group of captured Japanese were in a separate line. One wore an American soldier's army jacket. Most shivered with no shirts on. It rained cats and dogs. Some said that during one hour, at 5 pm, a record ten inches fell. I perspired terribly in my raincoat.

When the rain subsided, an unknown officer who finished chow stopped to talk with me. He asked about some of my few mechanical abilities and then said I should see him at the main base to work in his office. I did not go because I knew my officer, Mr. B, would never release me.

As more supplies began to arrive daily, I took notice of what was being unloaded, mainly 55-gallon drums filled with gasoline. Then a whole bunch of Budweiser beer, 24 bottles per case – 6,000 of them were unloaded about a half-block inland. They were guarded, and eventually distributed to all the units on base.

I recall one night I watched three guys put one whole case of beer on two logs tied together and floated it out to a sand bar a few hundred yards from shore. They drank in the moonlight. When it got very late, the tide came in and they had to swim back to the shore in deeper water as the sand bar disappeared.

There were some who had drinking problems and they watched for an opportunity to satisfy their desire. One took hydraulic fluid from equipment with the Seabees, mixed it with coke, drank it and died.

149

A story told by some surrendered Japanese on Manus:

- ○ March 30 – It was the eighth day since we began our withdrawal. We have been wandering around the mountain trails because of the enemy finding us. We struggled through heavy brush. All of our rations were depleted. Our bodies became completely exhausted. We got weaker and weaker and hungry, which became unbearable.
- ○ March 31 – Our walk continued with hopes of reaching Lorengau. We were lost in the mountains. We disposed of all our equipment and reluctantly our rifles also. It was torture every hour.
- ○ April 1 – We finally saw a native's shack and surrendered.

During the day we felt quite secure with aircraft securing the islands in our area. Every one of our military on the Admiralty Islands were trained to some degree to have combat with the enemy.

We began to receive unusable ammunition from ships in the harbor. Over twenty 12-inch diameter by 24-inch long bags containing black powder pellets were for us to get rid of. They were dumped at an isolated location near a small gulley. A small wood fire was made to burn them. Mack said we will roll them down into the fire one by one. I made a fuss about doing that because I had a mishap by doing just that with firecracker powder, and was burned.

"You will not refuse my order," was his remark.

When he rolled the first bag down into the fire, it blasted a huge flame back toward us that singed our hair, and my face felt the extreme heat. He said, "I thought that 30 feet away was far enough. That wasn't a good idea, we will try another way."

A small watercraft was ordered, we loaded it with the bags, sailed it out thirteen miles, and dumped them in the ocean.

About that time, our chief said we would move north down the beach about a mile to the Lugos Mission area. That place was named after a Methodist missionary who taught the natives some religion. Crudely painted signs that depicted their faith were hung on some trees in that area.

A New Boss and Progress

By May 18th, the Admiralty Islands were declared secured. Patrols continued around us on land, water and in the air until war's end.

Lugos Mission became the location where the naval ammunition depot started, without headquarters or an office to work from. Tents were put up on the hill in a swamp. We walked in boots and used cargo skids for walkways. Pete, Tom, Ray, Spoony and I shared a tent. Watch duty was no longer required at our area. Gunner Barnes, a warrant officer, took charge of us because our chief and Mack returned to the states for reasons unknown. Our new boss was about fifty years old and appeared to be in excellent physical shape. With his twenty-plus years spent in Naval Ordinance Service, I just knew he was not a generic leader. He taught us all about ordinance products. He explained with patience, and since we showed him some of our aggressive work abilities, he allowed us plenty of leeway in making decisions without him. He emphasized the importance of handling ammunition safely and working harder in order to end the war sooner.

Pete and I stood next to a pile of 5.38" projectiles. Beside them was a crate of fuses to use with them. Barnes said to be careful while handling them since a single one cost the price of a war bond – $18.75. It was the variable-time fuse, the first "smart missile" fuse. More enemy planes in the Pacific during World War Two were shot down using that fuse with the five-inch gun than with any other gun.

Gunner asked Pete to keep record of all the vessels' names and dates we served with ammunition in Seeadler Harbor. Gunner gave him a small, black book to do that. Then he drove off in his jeep – the Hurdy Gurdy he called it. He was the only expediter for our Lion Four ammunition services in the Pacific Ocean.

All he had was that little black book to work from. He drove back and forth all day long between ships and us on shore to keep things moving. Orders came to us daily requesting ammunition. Slowly, ships brought some from the states. When unloaded, our job was to store the ammo somewhere. We picked random areas in the jungle and covered them with tarpaulins. Only one truck was available to haul everything. Its wheels carved out paths into the jungle for new roadways. When in that dense jungle, it felt like another world, and we kept our rifles with us until work activity accelerated in that vicinity.

Pete and I worked as a team, and let the truck driver who brought the ammo help us unload. Approaching trucks could barely be heard in that thick brush.

The Seabees built seven 60x30 foot, ½-inch-thick steel Quonset ammunition shelters along the paths back in the jungle and covered them with soil. In about two weeks, enough growth was on them to where they were not seen from above.

Our need for trucks was critical. Finally, ships brought some. We acquired two – a Chevy two-ton, and a Mack 2-1/2 ton. None of us knew how to drive them. I was warned that the Mack truck had assisted powered air brakes. When used, the vehicle stopped on a dime. On my first use, I forgot and it stopped abruptly. My head hit the windshield, leaving me with a lump on my forehead. No seatbelts at that time. A diagram was stenciled on the dashboard to show the sequence required for shifting gears. The Chevy had to be double-clutched to move from gear to gear while driving.

With the amount of daily usage, abuse, and saltwater splashes on the vehicle, its life averaged about six months. One mechanic serving us became diabetic, and that left us to do the best we were able to with any vehicle problems.

We had only about forty men of the first echelon doing all the work and it became more hectic by the day. The second echelon came about six months later. The third and forth came near war's end. By that time, things were in full swing and on a fast roll. Some worked at a slower pace in all that heat.

Having no place to dock, the first supply ship had to remain anchored in the harbor for weeks. The Seabees worked continuously without faltering. They had many projects going on all over the Admiralty Islands. A dock was direly needed and as soon as possible. Besides the ongoing building projects, the Seabees also maintained and serviced what had been completed.

When they were building the dock, digging, trucking, and driving pilings into the coral of the shoreline took place for weeks. The road of coral was extended way out into the water and a dock was built atop it. It was large and long enough to dock two large ships. It was miraculously completed in a few short weeks and it has the shape of a letter T. Any type of vehicle could make turnarounds on it, some as large as twenty-ton trucks.

Once we saw a crane operator sluice his bucket of coral sideways too fast. When he stepped on the brakes to stop the swing at the dump site, it caused the crane to turn over. He was not injured, so we who witnessed it laughed.

The first ship that docked was really loaded. Its gross weight was about 7,000 tons. It sank low in the water, ammunition being its heaviest cargo. Our hard work began with unloading ammunition. We filled a landing craft (LCM), a 65-foot-long vessel. The LCM moved to shore, and we loaded the trucks from it. Gunner specified the areas where the truck unloaded in the rough of the jungle. There were no roads anywhere from the shoreline. The truck would make its way through the brush and mud and get about 3,000 yards inland for an unloading spot.

The Seabees plowed roads and built magazine shelters for the ammunition storage, which began at the end of that first short road. The muddy trails got covered with coral, which formed a hard surface for trucks to drive on.

Two of our group anxiously took the truck-driving jobs. George was from Georgia, and Bolger was from Texas. As drivers, it did not excuse them from assisting us with the loading and unloading of ammunition wherever it was.

When I saw how they drove, it appeared to me that it was their natural ability because they drove like insane hot-rodders, but they did their job well.

Gunner, who ran the show, plus the truck drivers, the

boatswain of the watercraft who loaded from the ship, and crews from other ships, kept us up to date with the latest information on most of the results of the invasions that took place and news of the ongoing war in the Pacific.

Pete and I were assigned to one magazine that was already filled with 5.38" powder casings. A truck drove up and it was George. He backed his truck against the magazine's open doors, jumped out of the truck and said, "I need fifty casings."

We loaded the truck with his assistance. Then he took off to the waiting ship, which was ready to depart. We had just filled that magazine two days ago.

Once I had a slight scare while removing casings from the pile in a magazine. A snake about three feet long slithered past me, off the pile, onto the ground, and outside the door. Right then I remembered what my friend, Perry, from South Carolina, told me. "If you see one, a mate will follow close by." Sure enough, at the last row of the pile, the other one slid past me and out the door.

The floors of the magazine were poured with non-sparking cement. It stayed damp all the time and was easily scratched by the metal containers. That was okay by me – no spark, no disaster.

I had to sync my mind to work, no two ways about it. An anemometer would measure zero if the air flow was checked. Thermometers read 100 degrees by eight in the morning. I perspired terribly, but the work had to be done. The moisture on my face mixed with my body salt and flowed into my eyes, and that burned. Wearing a headband helped, but that was too warm. Our containers of drinking water emptied fast and often.

159

Out in the Jungle

One day, my friend and partner Pete asked if I was hungry. It was past lunchtime and Gunner forgot about us. We were in the jungle, located at the magazine the most distant from the dock. That morning Gunner dropped us off with instructions to load a truck that would arrive for some 5.38" casings requested by a ship in the harbor. He left a .30-caliber rifle with ammunition. I placed it against the outside magazine wall for quick use if necessary. We still had some fear of any unknown person or animal.

Pete went across the road into the thick brush right up to a large banana plant, cut a whole stock of it, and brought it to me. We ate some. This was good since we had no lunch. We had been told to not take or remove any edible item from the grounds as it was the natives' livelihood, but we were hungry.

It was so quiet that I imagined hearing snakes sliding in the brush. Pete said to me, "I was so far in the think that I saw and heard the jungle grow."

"Okay, Pete, show me," I said.

He then told me, "Go in the brush and kneel down next to some thick plant, then stare at it without blinking your eyes for a minute and you will see it grow. Then press your ear to it and you will hear the creaking sound of it growing."

I saw and heard exactly what he told me with my own eyes and ears.

We Explored

It was my first walk down the beach. Some of the ground was of a reddish-brown gumbo. Along the eastern side of Manus, at the Lugos Mission area, there were yellow, red, and black sand beaches. The sand color identified the yellow beach, the red clay identified the red beach, and black stones pulverized by the buffeting waves made the black beach. The black beach appeared as one large, shiny black jewel , the water flowing on it made it glisten. The three beaches were reference points to invade the island of Manus.

At the red beach are where puddles of rain and salt water mixed, wild orchids grew. It surprised me that certain elements of nature would produce such beauty in ugly mud next to the path along the oceanside. We glorified them and then walked on them like they were ordinary weeds. Would folks at home believe that?

Along that same shoreline were remnants of the dead enemy's clothing partially buried in the ground. Also the smell of decay made the air smell like a skunk's discharge. At that moment it felt as though a battle had just ended. A small landing barge of the enemy's remained in the water, sunk and falling apart. Then came the sight of the river, which became our swimming place from then on, when time permitted.

In some areas the bomb craters had water filling them, and they were a haven for mosquitos. The natives were hired to spray stagnant pools of water with some mixture of diesel fuel for one dollar a day. A two-man Navy team used a large drum and trapped mice in certain areas to check for disease carriers.

Pete and I took a walk down the beach and I saw a bazooka on the ground. It was a live one and I thought I would keep it as a souvenir. I had to disarm it. Pete looked closely as I released the firing pin spring. The pin hit him right in the forehead. I thought that it would become an issue. He sat on the ground for a while and all turned out okay, but he had a headache for a while. A puncture remained on his forehead and we talked about the incident many times.

Further down the beach we came to the river which the natives called Lik-lik. That was our recreation area most of the time. During another time while off duty, another buddy and I ventured up a hill through thick brush. My foot slipped on the slick clay so I grabbed what looked like a nice green vine to hold. It was not; it was a four-foot-long vine snake and it just fell to the ground as I let go of it. With a machete I kept hacking away at the tangled vines and then came across a large field of bright, green bamboo. It was so thick and the shoots grew so close to each other, it seemed impossible to pass through that section, which was also an uphill climb of about 45 degrees.

A choice had to be made: cut through the middle of it or go back down the hill and start a new direction uphill. I decided to cut through it. It was tough. I had to cut the shoots with an angular swing that left the green, pointed spears a foot high. It was a problem to spread those strong shoots apart to pass through. The hill was forty-five degrees of slippery, angular ground with wet clay. It was a struggle but we both made it to the top.

163

Over the hill we saw rows of beautiful, tall coconut trees in the straight lines of a plantation. They were undisturbed by the bombardment of the island invasion. Certain people in Holland had the rights for producing coconuts from those trees. Our government had to pay the owners one dollar for each tree that was destroyed or missing on the island because of our invasion.

Bungee Jumping

After walking on higher ground we came to a forest valley and saw one of two native boys swinging across a wide ravine on a vine connected to a eucalyptus tree. They were both Polynesian. Some Melanesian natives were also residents of the Admiralty Islands. One took hold of a long vine and handed it to me. I swung out over the ravine and enjoyed it. Then one tied the vine to himself, climbed up about twenty-five feet, and from a small platform in the tree he jumped out into space and down to the ground. The vine stretched on his body as he came within three feet of the ground. He unleashed the vine from his body, looked at me, and said, "You, you, you."

I said to him, "No, no, no."

Work Ahead I Did Not Expect

W e handled any ammunition that was used by the Navy. The .30-caliber and .50-caliber rounds were packed in wooden cases, weighing from 92 to 112 pounds. A metal box containing sixteen shells of 40mm size weighed from 111 to 132 pounds. The 3.5" cartridge weighed about 75 pounds. The 5" and 6" projectiles weighed from 25 to 65 pounds each. The throw-type depth charges and hedgehogs weighed about ten pounds each. The large depth charges, the 350- and the 700-pound ones required lifting equipment to handle them. We also dealt with the 100-, 250-, 500-, 1,000- and 2,000-pound blockbuster bombs. Pyrotechnic items cased in wooden boxes weighed about 25 pounds. Most of our work consisted of the 5.38" ammunition. Each projectile weighed about 25 pounds and the powder casing for it weighed about fifteen pounds.

These were most widely used by the majority of ships due to having the variable-time fuse adapted to it, which made it an accurate bullet. Our supply of those projectiles and casings enlarged quickly as they came from the USA.

Our group was formed with men from just about every state in the forty-eight. The pre-war sailors knew their duties very well. When we, the greenhorns, entered the war and mingled with them and worked on the same assignment, there was some friction in attitudes and ideas on how operations would be performed. Because of that problem, new ideas cropped up from the men, and that showed that we were not puppets. I think it helped the war effort.

We could not remember the names of everyone we worked with, so all had nicknames. The few names I knew were Kapo, Ski, Slick, and Hey You. If a blunder was made, it was a *SNAFU* – situation normal, all fouled up.

Things got better when the Quonset huts were built. Good sleeping quarters, a chow hall, a recreation center, and a latrine that included a hot-and-cold-water shower. A ping-pong table was in the recreation room, but it took up most of the floor space so letter-writing had to be done on the bunk beds. It became the Lugos Mission Village on top of the hill.

Refrigerating food was a problem for the cooks so we went on K rations once in a while. The most common meat served was mutton, which came from Australia. It was served with applesauce. Potatoes, eggs, and milk were made from a powder form. We missed fresh milk and ice cream. Fresh fruit and veggies were a rarity. Flour to make bread was often spoiled by moisture.

Once, I released an abnormal stool deposit. It was checked by our pharmacist and he determined that it was a lack of fruits and veggies. Within a few days, a new product arrived for us to drink. It was vegamato – V8. On the can's label it showed the contents having juice from several vegetables, two of which were celery and carrots. The drink tasted awful to me; without refrigeration, even worse. Coca-Cola was one drink many could not resist, and that was not good.

In the chow hut a fan blew over our heads, but it was still too warm for comfort so we always ate quickly and left. At times the food supply tightened so oatmeal was often served at breakfast. One morning, Hoppy sat next to me and we had oatmeal. He said to me, "Am I seeing things or is that something wiggling in my bowl?"

I and two sailors looked and one hollered, "Maggots!" When Hoppy heard that, he grabbed his mouth and went outside to heave.

We called the pharmacist, and as he looked in the bowl he said, "They won't hurt you." Most everyone dumped their oatmeal into the waste can. K-rations again. In a few days, a new load of food arrived from Australia and with it the usual meat – mutton. I liked to eat it with applesauce; it cut the fatty taste.

Seldom came a package of goodies from home. Tommy from Hayward, California, received most of them. He was generous and shared them with us.

We spent many days at the magazines, some far back in the jungle. The ammunition most of us used were the .30-calber rifle cartridges, .50-caliber for the machine guns, the 20mm, the 40mm, and 5.38" used in the anti-aircraft guns.

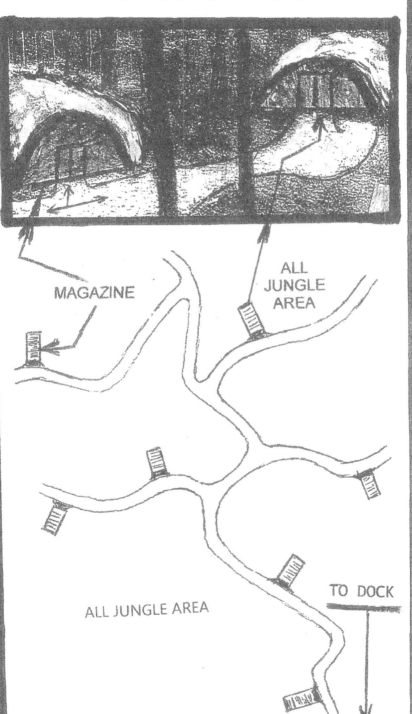

STORAGE MAGAZINES IN JUNGLE

MAGAZINE

ALL JUNGLE AREA

ALL JUNGLE AREA

TO DOCK

A truck would pull up to the doors of the magazine. We placed a roller rack onto the truck bed, with the other end on the ammunition pile of the magazine. We pushed the boxes on the rollers, one-by-one, into the truck.

Pete the truck driver and I were able to load a truck with 105 cases, each one weighing 112 pounds, in ten minutes when we felt like it. The normal time for that operation usually took 20-25 minutes. The 40mm cases weighed as much as 132 pounds, requiring two to handle them. Those steel cases got very hot in the sun and were more difficult to handle.

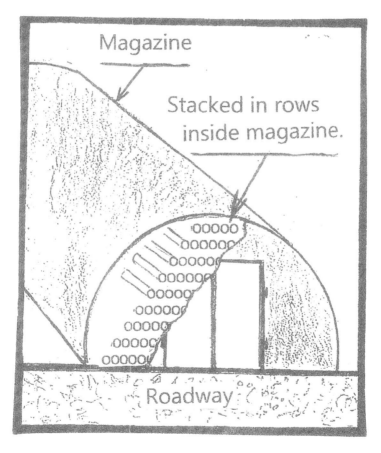

As Bolger backed his truck to the magazine door one morning, I walked behind the truck to get to the other side as it rolled back. As it did, I got pinned between the truck and the magazine. My body got squeezed, but I got out and was not injured, although my chest hurt for days. I thought there was enough space there for me to get through. It was a very close call. I felt so stupid by doing that. Then I thought, what if I became a statistic with my life ending, would the report going to my folks read KIA – Killed In Action?

A Captain's Mast

This was a preliminary hearing that was held on account of a wrongdoing by three of us. An officer charged us with negligence in handing ammunition.

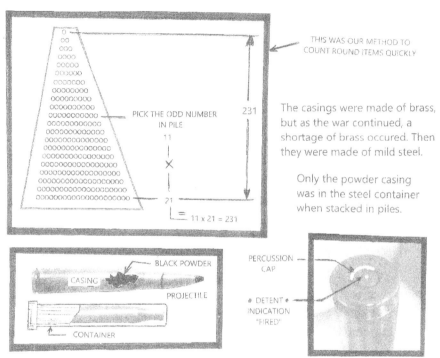

THIS WAS OUR METHOD TO COUNT ROUND ITEMS QUICKLY

PICK THE ODD NUMBER IN PILE

231

11

×

21

11 x 21 = 231

0
00
000
0000
00000
000000
0000000
00000000
000000000
0000000000
00000000000
000000000000
0000000000000
00000000000000
000000000000000
0000000000000000
00000000000000000
000000000000000000
0000000000000000000
00000000000000000000
000000000000000000000

The casings were made of brass, but as the war continued, a shortage of brass occured. Then they were made of mild steel.

Only the powder casing was in the steel container when stacked in piles.

BLACK POWDER

CASING

PROJECHLE

CONTAINER

PERCUSSION CAP

◆ DETENT ◆ INDICATION "FIRED"

Our gunner had driven us to the dock where an officer stood next to a pile of 5.38" powder casings being readied for loading onto a watercraft which was to go to his ship in the harbor. Spoony, Warner, and I loaded the truck that was delivered there. The officer pointed out to us that the lid of one container with a casing of powder in it was poorly secured, and said, "It might fall out and explode." For that reason, we were told to appear at a captain's mast the next morning dressed in clean work clothes at 9 a.m. in the officers' quarters.

We attended, and each of us were asked not once, but twice, who was to be blamed for the wrongdoing. No one answered. Then a harsh reprimand was given to us by the conducting officer with a closing statement: "Brig time if that occurs again. You are now dismissed."

As we walked out and our gunner sympathized with us on that stringent warning but mentioned to us to be more careful from then on.

All three of us agreed that we did not want to go through that again. One loose binding was even too much, but with the enormous amount of ammunition that we handled, it just happened.

The Seabees were a hard-working bunch. They planned and constructed most of their projects without much engineering because they had experience in doing things the most logical ways, and successfully accomplished what was needed. A spot was picked on the hill of the Lugos Mission area for our living quarters. A constant ocean breeze flowed through the open walls of our Quonset hut. After completing a hard day's work, we showered and then laid on our bunks until chow time. Gentle waves bouncing against the shoreline could be seen and heard from our cots. Sometimes I fell asleep and missed dinner.

A road next to camp led down to the river where our leisure time was often spent. Bud and I were the ones seen there most of the time because we swam a lot. The steep climb on the gravel path back up to our hut was a bit of a drudgery, but the enjoyment we had was every bit worth it.

Our post office address became NAVY 3205. It was also the code the military used to know our location, which was not advertised to anyone. Mail was brought in to us about every two weeks by a Douglass DC-3 cargo plane, which was escorted into our security zone by a fighter plane. Several times, an enemy plane flew within the screen of the mail plane, but was caught in time and never got into our island area. No one ever missed mail call.

Ever see a sick cat? Well, some people looked that way when they received no mail.

The cost of airmail was three cents. For those in the military who served overseas, there was a free mailing service called V-mail; Victory mail. The envelope was three inches by five with a sheet of paper in it, and was available at any post office without cost. Nothing extra was allowed to be added inside of the envelope. The mail was censored somewhere down the line. When someone used airmail, our immediate officer censored those. I wrote some letters in Lithuanian to my folks, and since my officer was not able to read them, he had me swear before him that I did not have anything in my writing to jeopardize our security. On the one, small sheet allowed in the V-mails, many wrote in tiny lettering in order to put more on paper to send home.

When I was overseas, my older brother served with General Patton's army in Europe. He sent me V-mails frequently. When receiving some from him, they had pieces of writing cut out by the censor with a razor blade. I mentioned that to him and later I learned the reason for it.

In his writing, he made a comparison of both our overseas duties and I remember him telling me how completely different our

173

two wars were.

All of my friends were in military service, so I had only my parents to write to.

Spoony was a jolly guy who bragged constantly about his girlfriend back home. Then the mail from her stopped arriving and he became very solemn. He checked with his parents back home about it. He received an answer from them that changed his life. Before entering the Navy, he made lots of money as a lumberjack in the state of Washington. He, with his girlfriend, saved money together in the bank for when they got married. Well, she took off with all their savings and no word was heard from her. Spoony, a man who was bold and stronger than any of us, developed a sheepish attitude. Some aimed derogatory remarks about him from that information he related to us.

We Needed Help

By the end of 1944, the third and fourth echelons of Lion Four landed on Manus Island. We received more help with the gunners group to serve ammunition. The population of our group enlarged all of a sudden, but we also were greatly pounded with more work. Many had long hair and there was no barber anywhere. I was coerced into doing haircutting. Things became more hectic for me. I cut hair in the recreation room when time permitted. Lieutenant B. asked me to do it full-time, but I refused because I was ready to take my exam for the promotion to Gunners Mate 3/c Petty Officer. I studied many days preparing for the test, as exhausted as I was from my daily duties. For the promotion, I had to pass three parts of the test. I showed that the physical duties, were performed properly, at least 32 of the 40 questions of the written test I answered correctly, and then with an interview with the gunnery officer, I convinced him that I was ready for the promotion. A time interval of six months between promotions was required, and only if an opening was available. Most promotions were easily made because we were in such actions that made more openings for gunners as the war continued.

As I passed, it made me more available for transfer without notice. Being a petty officer, I was assigned to supervise a crew of eight men. My promoting officer was quite strict and some vulgarity was heard from him by some men.

A small vehicle was assigned to Pete and me for use to transport men in any work area between the dock and the ammunition storages that were scattered throughout the area. Pete and I took care of all the requests by ships that came to Manus for ammunition in preparation for island invasions north of us. When new members joined our groups, our burden eased and we were a bit relieved.

The new members complained about the torture from the very hot sun when their labor was required. They were slow. When I mentioned being on the island for over a year, they began to cooperate in a more aggressive manner. They volunteered their efforts more abundantly, and soon it began to look like a huge industrial development with men who worked as busily as bees.

Our New Lion Four Commander

Our first commander was Hopper. Then there was Commander Cunneen, builder of the ammunition depot, then Jones, who conducted the very busiest months of our activities until war's end. Commander Jones spent too much of his time with us by observing our activities and at the same time making improvements in the methods we used in the handling of ammunition. He saw what a laborious toil it was for us daily, and decided we needed more time for rest and recreation.

He picked a spot close to camp for a baseball field. He had it cleared of all obstacles and the area was flattened out by dragging a bed spring tied behind a vehicle. He had a carpenter build a small shelter in back of home plate. After the diamond was laid out, he played ball with us – a man in his fifties.

I remember how different he was from most officers. He did not exhibit his superiority to us, but that pin on the collar of his shirt was the indicator that showed his rank. His shirt sleeves were rolled up most of the time. He was a big man, weighing about 175 and very agile in his movements. Everyone seemed to like him and willingly obeyed his orders.

When the war ended, as he left he said, "Come to see me if you need a job. I will be with the Memphis Power and Light Company. I will hire any of you."

The work load became heavier and heavier. The main base at Lorengau and the surrounding areas of the Admiralty Islands were in good shape to serve the fleets inside the harbor. We provided the ammunition service and the other divisions of Lion Four supplied the fleets with their services and equipment. Cargo and ammunition continually flowed in from the good ole people of the USA who worked hard and sacrificed their time and efforts to help with the war. Some had names marked on products we received. Some got smashed during shipment due to improper packaging and some never showed up for some unknown reason. I called Manus the Bank Island. The fighting ships returned from the fighting zones for replenishment of ammunition and supplies almost daily, which kept us very busy.

Natives had jungle rot, but we encountered ringworm, which was a constant threat in that heat. It is a round, red ring with tiny blisters (vesicles) that hold clear, watery fluid. It itched badly from scratching and would spread easily. Some developed it so badly that they were sent home for treatment. I had small ring patches in my armpits and crotch. Lots of willpower was required to refrain from scratching. Our pharmacist gave us pure alcohol to scrub it. Fresh-water bathing often helped but so much free time was not abundant. I did my best and after a few weeks it cleared completely, though it left scars.

Explosion of the USS Mount Hood

T he *USS Mount Hood* (AE-11) was launched on November 28, 1943, in North Carolina. Commissioned on July 1, 1943, officers and enlisted men totaled 318.

Length 459 ft.
Beam 63 ft.
Draft 28 ft.
Speed 16 knots

Armament: 1 5.38" gun
4 3.5" guns
2 40mm AA guns
10 20mm AA guns

At Norfolk, Virginia, the Mount Hood was loaded with ammunition. It transited through the Panama Canal on August 27, 1944, and immediately sailed to Finschafen, New Guinea. It left there and arrived at Seeadler Harbor in Manus Island. It was assigned to the Southwest Pacific Command. It anchored in about 19 fathoms of water with a load of about 3,800 tons of explosives aboard.

On November 10, 1944, while Zooky and I had breakfast together in the chow hut, he asked if I would cut his hair. It hung over his ears a lot. I agreed, and we decided to go down to the oceanside, find a log to sit on, and cut his hair. It was a bright, sunny morning and very hot, but some breeze came off the lake, which felt good.

As I was cutting Zooky's hair, one of our small fighter planes flew over us at cruising speed. Suddenly, a huge black cloud of smoke rose above the water right in the center of the harbor. Connected to a small ball of smoke was a much larger one, and that entire black cloud was an explosion that mushroomed 7,000 feet in the air, obscuring the surrounding vicinity for a radius of about 500 yards in every direction. One small blast of air hit us, and then the second, a huge wave of air, followed immediately, knocking us both down to the ground, but did not injure us. Our first thought was that it was an enemy attack so we ran into the jungle for cover. A few minutes later we saw our planes scouring the sky, and then we felt safe. With about thirty minutes gone by, all was as quiet as ever in the entire harbor area. We ran up the hill and then got the news that in the harbor, the *USS Mount Hood* exploded.

The ship and all who were on it – 295 men – had disappeared in six seconds. Fragments from it were hurled as far as 2,000 yards over the water. The force of the explosion blasted a trough in the ocean floor more than one-hundred yards long, fifty feet wide, and between thirty and forty feet deep, directly below the position of the ship. Over forty vessels were damaged or sunk by the flying debris – the ARG-3, DE-344, AKA-9, YMS-293, YMS-238, YMS-49, YMS-340, YMS-286, YMS-243, ARG-6, YMS-39, YMS-71, YMS-81, YMS-140, YMS-319, YMS-335, ATF-109, AD-17, DE-412, YMS-1, AG-31, AO-52, IX-131, TF-681, YMS-52, YO-77, AK-51, ARS-8, DD-580, DD-744, APD-7, CVE-82, DE302, YMS-342, CVE-80, YMS-39, and thirteen small boats damaged beyond repair. Also, 33 other small craft had some damage. There were about 200 vessels in the harbor at the time.

On that bright, early morning, a young Naval Reserve lieutenant and thirteen enlisted men climbed over the side of the Mount Hood and down into a small boat that took them to shore. While on shore a few minutes later, one sailor looked back and saw smoke, then hollered, "Look, our ship just went up in smoke!"

Right at that moment, they were all knocked to the ground. They got back into the small boat but only saw debris all over the water. After observing the massive amount of scattered, floating remnants of the ship's sections, they returned to the beach.

They had come in to pick up mail, some communication manuals, a few men needed dental work, and I heard that one was being taken to the base brig.

The *USS Mindanao* was the closest ship to the explosion. It had 33 holes in it above the waterline. One- to ten-foot holes were seen in the bulkheads. One of the Mount Hood's gun mounts shot off and ripped right through the stack of the Mindanao. Men who were standing topside facing toward the explosion were killed outright.

On the starboard side of the Mindanao's quarterdeck, 32-year-old seaman Arthur Kephart was washing down the bulkheads in preparation for inspection. Suddenly, he saw metal flying all around and over his head, with the steel bulkheads folding like paper before his eyes. He could not see anything around the deck for a while as the air filled with black smoke.

Some 221 pieces of debris, ranging up to 150 pounds, careened off the USS Argonne's portside into the water alongside the ship. Some steel landed on the yard freighter (YF-681) and the yard oiler (Yo-77), whose oil hoses were still attached. Its fresh water and saltwater lines were ruptured.

The *USS Piedmont*, about 3,500 yards away, had its fire and rescue parties dispatched to assist the nearby vessels, even though it had fragments of steel that hit its superstructure and ricocheted off its bulkheads and decks.

Help was not long in coming to assist those in need with their injuries on the Mindanao. The first ship that arrived was the *USS President Hayes*, a troop transport that just unloaded men in the Philippines area. The first to climb aboard was the doctor and five corpsmen, and soon more help came.

One of the corpsmen who climbed aboard described what he saw. Lots of confusion, about 75 percent casualties, and many in shock. As they administered treatment with morphine, sulfa drugs, and battle dressings, they saw dead all around them. It took half an hour for plasma to arrive. A few had received concussions and could not catch their breath. One corpsman said, "Seen by me was one officer's body torn in half."

Some were alive, but their arms and legs were gone, and some had steel stuck in their bodies and holes in their stomachs, and they patiently waited for help. Some with quivering lips tried to say something but could not. Since they did not have enough strength, they did not relate very clearly. They probably wanted to say, I am still alive."

The medical team did all they were able to, and more help came on the way as they left. While going back to shore, the saw a minesweeper with its entire superstructure blown off and only blood on its decks.

One of the first shore-based medical men to do the job of removing the dead was Hunter Gammon. As he climbed aboard, a chief had already prepared a winch to lower remains covered with white sheets and tagged. They were lowered into a tugboat below. When Hunter was done, he left the ship with the clothes he wore, which looked dipped in blood.

On shore he took a shower and then went to assist those needing help in the base hospital operating room. After some agonizing hours, and being very exhausted, he left for bed.

The same day, Commodore Boak ordered a complete investigation into the disaster. Three days later, on Monday, November 13th, after hearing all the gathered evidence, the session closed with a conclusion that ruled out the possibility of a submarine or air attack because of insufficient evidence. The conclusion arrived with a decision that said the initial explosion probably resulted from a load of ammunition dropped into or struck against a hatch in the #3 or #4 hold of the ship.

A ship fitter by the name of Roark was at that time lowering some welding equipment over the side to a smaller vessel from his ship, which faced the Mount Hood. He saw it lift out of the water as it exploded, and broke into three sections that disintegrated into smaller pieces that flew through the air. The first section was the bow section up to the bridge. The second section was the bridge and a portion behind it, and the rest was the fantail. All three sections split during the second, larger explosion. Roark was knocked down, but only felt dazed. He crawled under the boat deck and looked all over himself. His arm had been hit and was useless. He looked for a corpsman and found one as he passed through a darkened hatchway, only lit by an emergency light. He was rendered aid, given a shot, and his forehead marked with an iodine swab with the letter M. He lost his arm and had an injured leg. His next move was to wait for some transportation to take him home.

In the late afternoon, we asked Gunner if help was needed at the base hospital or elsewhere. He said there was enough help but to check in the morning. After next morning's breakfast, the three of us – Zooky, Walter, and I – walked the long trail to the hospital at Lorengau Beach. As we entered the building, there were two medics standing inside. We asked if blood or help were needed. They said more than enough was already offered and taken care of, and things were getting back into proper order. We walked out and shuffled along the shoreline, gazing out at where the Mount Hood had been anchored in the harbor.

A sailor nearby told us he was knocked down, and told us

about how he saw the coconut trees bend so far down from the explosion that they almost kissed the ground. The koala bears fell out of their nestings and three-foot-high waves flowed quite a way inland and left a mess.

We walked the shoreline, discussing the awful tragedy. Warner said to us, "Look down there at the water's edge. It looks like small pieces of flesh to me." When I looked at what was mixed in with the sand, I said a prayer immediately. Information was announced to all on Manus that a church service would be held on Sunday to pray for all those lost or injured from that disaster. Many attended.

I knew of five ships with ammunition that exploded during World War Two: The SS Quinault and the SS E. A. Bryan at Mare Island, California, while loading in July, 1944, losing all men aboard. The *USS Mount Hood* at Manus Island, also lost all men aboard. The *SS Burke* was hit by a kamikaze that killed all men aboard in December, 1944, at sea while at Mindoro in the Philippines. The *SS Serpens* exploded at Guadalcanal in January, 1945. Of all the ships that exploded carrying ammunition, the *USS Mount Hood* was the worst disaster.

News of those disasters traveled quickly across the entire Pacific Ocean among the sailors. It also made us more aware of the danger in doing our job of handling ammunition. I was surprised that the only complaint was the hard work in that terrible heat that continued for so long until the war's end.

About two years after the war, while employed by the Rock Island Railroad and working in their Chicago office, two of my coworkers; Bob, a Navy veteran and John, an Army veteran, rode home on the train with me each evening. It was about a half-hour ride. Neither of them had served overseas. Together we told war stories. We kept our conversations toned down as we talked, but not enough. When it was mentioned that I witnessed the explosion of the Mount Hood that disappeared with all men in about six seconds, people in about five seats on the train focused their eyes strenuously at me. It scared me so badly that I made up my mind to stop telling Navy stories.

In 2012, one Navy buddy somehow got mail to me when we lived in Missouri. He invited me to a reunion of the Lion Four group at Claire, Michigan. I attended, and there they said they were clams like me. They turned their lives around by writing some of their experiences for family and friends. That gave me my inspiration to do something about it.

As we continued talking, Bob said to me, "I have the *Our Navy* magazine dated February, 1945, which I subscribe to. Pages 12 and 13 has the picture and complete story which you just described. That Monday, he brought me the magazine and gave it to me for keeps.

More than Halfway to Japan

We were 3,750 miles from home. Tokyo was 2,340 miles away. The reception on the Japanese radio was poor. Even with the crackling noise, we were all ears. The Japanese broadcast messages to demoralize the American troops, announcing propaganda along with songs such as, "Don't You Wish You Were Home?" It was all to break down one's fighting mood. Some leaflets were dropped by air. One was like this:

BEWARE OF THE TRIPLE THREAT

Hi Joe, I sure hate to be in your shoes. Your commander certainly chose a beehive place for you to land. Don't you know what dangers confront you at Mindoro? They are tamaraw (small, silky, killer buffaloes), the malaria-ridden mosquitos, and the Japanese soldiers.

The tamaraw are the fiercest animals on earth, and only found in Mindoro. When you march through the jungle, look out, they come at you unaware and you are dead before you even know what even hit you.

The mosquitos are master-monster malaria bombers. They don't give a damn when or where they hit, and once they do, you are definitely a goner. And the Japanese soldiers are even worse. We don't have to tell you about that, you should know about them.

By the way, if you do get into Mindoro, the mina de oro means a mine of gold. If you dig for some, and deep enough, it will become your grave.

With all those scares, our troops just laughed them off. It did not hinder their mood to fight at all.

That radio program came on very close to bedtime.

The Stage For the Philippine Islands Invasion

A large convoy of about 500 vessels anchored in and outside of Seeadler harbor in Manus. I saw every type, large and small. They were all loaded up and ready to go for a large invasion.

It was announced on the ships and on shore that a religious service would be held at 10 a.m. on the Lorengau beach the morning of the convoy's departure.

As I joined the attendance, many of us who neglected church services in the past came joyfully but with concern. It was time to give out transfers after the service. We asked each other, "What are you doing here?"

Everyone had the same answer. "Same reason you are!" A close buddy of mine – Paul, a torpedoman – was transferred from Lion Four onto the *USS Jenkins.*

The service was so satisfying. It was a place where everyone was treated the same. No individual was treated special. No cliques or elites came to show their important position. My thought was that it should be practiced more often. It lasted about half an hour. At about noon, an hour after services, one by one the ships left the harbor area in a parade fashion out to sea. A few ships sounded their loud horns and some toot-toots were heard from smaller vessels as they left.

When the harbor emptied, it appeared as a large lagoon. Our workload quickly lessened dramatically, which left us more time for rest and recreation.

After several weeks, some ships returned from the battlefront requiring an ammunition refill. With them they brought news of the fighting that took place.

It was the leadership of General MacArthur with his troops and Admiral Nimitz's Navy that invaded Leyte during January, 1945. It was captured with 120,000 men, with 3,500 killed and 11,900 wounded.

The invasion of Manila then took place in February, 1945, and lasted one month. It was the bloodiest war in the Pacific. Our loss was 17 battleships, 11 cruisers, 19 destroyers, and some submarines and aircraft. Thirty-five-hundred of our troops fought, and 3,000 Filipinos assisted. Forty-six large transport vessels with hundreds of merchant men were lost in the campaign.

One horrendous situation that ended was the enslavement of the Bataan prisoners. They were enslaved and tortured between 1939 and 1945 by Japanese General Tomoyuki Yamashita. Some survived, but many died young as the result of poor health that was sustained during their torture.

I Met Neighbors From Home

As the war continued, more areas on Manus were cleared to erect Quonset huts, which were needed for storage and protective shelters of the present operating facilities. The Seabee equipment operators cleared a section of land up on the hill a bit over a mile from our Lugos Mission village. For a few days in June of 1945, in the 115-degree heat, they plowed brush and red clay to level the ground with their bulldozers.

At about the same time, I received a letter from my brother, telling me a neighbor of ours was at a Seabee construction site which was vaguely described by me. He said to look for a lanky, thirty-year-old bulldozer operator named Al from Dolton, Illinois. Two days after receiving that information, I decided to walk through the rough trails to that working site. Al was told to watch for me, with my description as a shrimpy nineteen-year-old sailor with blue eyes. I found the spot where bulldozers were sputtering away, busy as ever. I spotted him, taller than the other two operators. He saw me walk up to his machine and he shut it off. We talked a lot, then he asked me if I would like to try his machine. Before I answered, he picked me up and placed me in the driver's seat. With the start-up of the noisy diesel engine, he said, "Try it." I tried pushing some of that red clay but did not do too well. I had to stretch my body to reach the pedals on the floor and manipulate levers to coordinate movements of that machine. It did not suit me too well, so I told him he could have his monster back as I jumped off of it.

I thought that area would be cleared for buildings. Soon, I found out I was wrong. A few days later, tents were set up in that area. Warner and I walked there and saw soldiers occupying them. They were dressed in khakis, but none had patches or markings on their clothing to identify their company or rank. Some facts poured out from the rumor mill that, since refusing orders given to them to perform their last assignment by their superiors, they were placed there awaiting a court martial trial.

However, it felt so good to see someone special from home. We had never met before. After the war, my brother arranged a meeting of Al and I with a surprise visit at a local tavern. Three together, we and the other veterans shot the bull late into the night, drinking away

Another Neighbor From Home

A crew of raw recruits of their ship came straight from California to Manus. It was a scheduled stop to load up with ammunition for use in the forward areas of the battlefront. They were so white they appeared anemic to me. They must have sat in the shade on their ship all the way over. We had no shade on our ship. Five came in a truck right from the dock to where Spoony and I worked. We began loading .50-caliber cartridges, each box weighing 112 pounds, onto the truck. On their faces was a reluctance to assist us in filling the order. They were dressed neatly in their Navy blue working clothes with their white hats. We wore commando greens, the cuffs on our trousers rolled up, our sweaty, sweaty bodies perspiring continuously.

All of the sudden, one turns to me and says, "I Know you, you live in Roseland."

I studied his face for a few seconds then shouted, "Johnny, my grammar-school buddy." Soon, all of our attitudes coordinated together more pleasantly and the truck got filled in no time at all.

Then he says to me, "How could you stand to work in this horrible climate?"

My answer to him, "It's been over a year already."

Six sailors came from a destroyer for ammunition. They refused to load ammo with us for their order, stating, "We only work on our ship." That upset me.

Well, they sat on their butts only a short while. Gunner showed up, then they moved their butts quickly to assist us, anxious to get back to their ship.

Jungle Becomes Base Under Seabees Magic

John McCullough, Inquirer, Washington Bureau – January 1945

Nine months ago, the Admiralty Islands was a mangrove swamp infested with Japanese. Today, by virtue of the First Cavalry Division and the incredible ingenuity of the Seabees, it is one of the most powerful naval bases in the world. Nowhere in the Pacific, with the possible exception of Guam, is the fantastic power which the United States Navy's marshalling to crush Japan so astoundingly exemplified.

Get out your map. If it is a fairly recent one, you will see a few little dots in the Bismarck Sea, about halfway between Dutch New Guinea and the upper end of New Ireland, just south of the equator, is Manus.

Properly speaking, Manus is Navy terminology for the vast Seeadler harbor, encircled by Manus and Los Negros Islands, sheltered windward by the chain of palm-fringed atolls.

Aside from a remote airstrip on Los Negros Island, taken last March by the First Cavalry and by whose coral sweep the first buried its dead, the Japanese did very little to develop Manus, Los Negros, as a fleet anchorage. They had an embarrassment of naval riches. But some shrewd eye in the United States Navy, we were told is was Admiral William Halsey, Jr. frosty-eyed nemesis of Nippon, who spotted Manus, placed a peremptory finger upon it and said, "That's the place."

It is a place, fantastic as some tall tale from the Arabian Nights. Aladdin's Lamp and the magic carpet both operated here under the better-known name of the United States Navy construction battalion – the immortal Seabees.

Our group of eight naval correspondents from Washington have gape-mouthed through the forward areas of the Pacific, but I think our jaws developed the most extensive sag here. The statistics alone are stunning.

On June 8, 1944, there was not a single American-erected building of any kind on Manus or Los Negros Island. By September

194

15th, there were 3,100 Quonset huts spread across the sloping hills for miles, and 969 supply warehouses crowding the busy harbor ledge.

The same Seabees which created a short establishment of Espiritu Santo, which supported the invasion of the Solomon Islands, moved to Manus.

In those months they built over 450 miles of three-lane highways, comparable to Pennsylvania's superhighway. Construction of a high lift pumping station delivering 4,000,000 gallons of pure cold water a day. Incredible in the Pacific forward areas.

This was Uncle Sam rolling up his sleeves, mad as a hornet. Who said it couldn't be done? One of the greatest and most speedy jobs of construction and base organizations in our naval history.

As we steamed down the harbor under the roaring tropical rainfall, the great anchorage seemed alive with ships. They extended hull down beyond the horizon, with only tips of their masts visible. Every type, from battle wagons to harbor tugs, busily running around along their busy, diverse errands. On the floating docks were sparks from welding torches all through the night. All size vessels were repaired on those monster docks, all day and all night around the clock.

The escorting officer apologetically mentioned that this harbor usually had three times that amount of vessels in for one reason or another. Seeadler Harbor, called the "inner harbor," is only nine miles long and three miles wide. The harbor itself is fifty miles long and in some places fourteen miles wide.

The surgical facilities would be such a pleasure for some to *work in as they had such well-groomed surroundings and equipment kept up-to-date by the strong-backed corpsmen.*

This vast harbor was equipped with gangway lights, powerful searchlights, and the blinking of signal lights from shore to shore and shore to ship, all night long.

Night and day, winches whining, clanking, and puffing, moved cargo on or off the ships preparing for its next trip out to sea, another invasion or leaving for home. Iron-lunged sailors continuously prodding help within their work assignments, natives moving along in their skittish robes and with bare feet, humming tunes as they worked.

The jungle smell was enjoyed in the night breeze blown from the plants such as orchids and grassy growth filled the air pleasantly. It was sickening to think that all of this will return, some day, to the primitive design of nature as it was before the war started.

I remember that late evening very well. Early that day, word was spread that a touring group of high-ranking officers are around making observations on the Admiralty Islands. Four of us decided to see who they were. In the evening we tracked them down to being on Los Negros. We stayed our distance and saw them watching the natives working on the docks. It was the first time I saw high-ranking officers on the islands. One interesting site was watching the natives loading sacks of potatoes on trucks. It reminded me of our typical labors.

Keep It Going

That definitely was our aim. Most of us had that aggressive attitude with some prompting by our gunner. He always remarked, "Work hard and get it over with." He trusted us a lot. He left us for days at a time and we had to use our own judgment pertaining to unexpected situations quite often. We continually filled ships' orders requiring ammunition while taking short rest periods. Any time Gunner spent with us, the conversation was entirely on explosives. With his instruction plus what I learned in the states, my main interest was to disarm explosives. I learned two ways to do bombs with their fuse or detonator intact.

From day to day, we not only supplied ships that needed ammo, but we also took their unusable explosives. We piled those on the ground in an area of our choice and covered them with tarpaulins. Days later, we loaded them on a landing barge, sailed ten miles from shore, and then hand-by-hand threw each one over the side in the deep sixty.

At the age of eighteen, I never envisioned that the work I would be doing would be so difficult, demanding, and dangerous. My thoughts were continually on how long I would last.

It all got worse. Promises that the remainder of the Lion Four gunners joining us soon to help proved to not be accurate; it was weeks before they came. More ships entered the harbor needing ammunition. Our workload became heavier by the day and we went to bed each night as exhausted as ever.

One day, our personnel transport vehicle was not available, so that morning the first truck to be filled with ammo brought Spoony, Pete and me to the farthest magazine in the jungle, over two miles from the dock. From 9 a.m. to 3 p.m., we filled truck after truck with 5.38" powder casings, emptying all that was in the magazine. More was requested on the order, but no more was available.

Each driver that came for a load brought a container of drinking water for us. It was a regular thing wherever we worked. There was no water at our site. When the last truck filled and left, we were forgotten out there in that hot, sunny, 115-degree heat without drinking water. We got very thirsty and looked around for some broad-leafed plants that might have had moisture on them, but found none. We rested in a shady section of the magazine, but that was not satisfying. We walked around on the coral road in circles, listening intently for the sound of a vehicle. The quiet prevailed, except for a small group of the most beautiful birds I have ever seen, chirping their tunes through the sky closely over our heads. Perspiration ran down my body, carrying salty deposits that formed in my trousers that showed a wide, white, belt-like line all around my waist. The salted crusted and caked so stiffly in the cloth, my pants would stand erect like a board.

Pete laughed. "Let me see!" I removed my pants and stood them erect on the ground. I had taken too many salt pills without enough water, which caused some dizziness then got worse. My skin dried and my tongue and lips swelled. My energy was so drained that it became difficult to speak clearly. All three of us felt about the same. Occasionally we glanced at each other pitifully.

We thought about walking back to our village but knew it would be a long struggle. We felt confident that help would arrive soon, but it had been hours since the last loaded truck left.

Eventually, a truck came and the driver had water for us. It was our good ol' buddy Bolger, a Texan and the best driver in our unit.

We anxiously drank the ice-cold water, taking small sips to avoid a possible convulsion. After regaining some strength, we climbed into the truck. It took only a few minutes for the driver to take us to the chow hall. After a good dinner and enough to drink, we rested and discussed the tough day we had.

Gunner kept record of all the vessels we served with explosives. On the pages of his little black book he noted the names and numbers of the ships and the military units and dates we served with ammunition.

Duties weighed on Gunner so tremendously that he decided to give Pete that book. The following day we were shocked to hear Gunner was suddenly transferred, and left us.

At that same time, the war ended in Europe. Our ships came to the Pacific Ocean from the Atlantic during June-July 1945. That increased our workload as battles continued on the Pacific front.

Some battleships, cruisers, and aircraft carriers that came into harbor had their hulls painted camouflage. When I first saw one, I had to look twice to know what it was – a section of land or a vessel on the water.

A new officer was assigned to our gunners group. He was very educated through schooling in the states, but he had no actual
200

time working with field-experienced men. The heat affected him so he was not seen often, and that left us on our own, doing our own thing, which helped operations run smoothly. It was obvious that our Lion Four commander did not favor him as a functional leader.

A small Quonset hut was built in the immediate living area of our Lugos Mission village. It was an office building where formal paper requisitions were typed up with all of our operating transactions. It became a very busy time for us.

Pete and I had the most field experience, so Lieutenant S said one of us had to take the office job. All four echelons of Lion Four, already located on Manus, operated efficiently in the field.

When the war ended in Europe, all the ships that came to the Pacific Ocean to assist increased our work load quite a bit.

Pete insisted I take the job in the office because he knew I had some office experience with paperwork. I immediately resisted, saying, "You were in the Navy longer than I, so you deserve to get that job."

After plowing through five minutes of a struggling conversation, he then said, "Okay, I'll take it. Then he removed the little black book from his pocket and handed it to me. I continued, as accurately as possible, to record the dates and names of the vessels we served until the war ended. No one ever asked or even cared for the book, so I ended up with it.

Many years went by and I still had that book, but it was frayed, so I decided to copy all its contents onto sheets of paper. It filled four pages. As computers became available and I could explore events through the internet, I found and read where and what those ships accomplished with the ammunition we served them. It was interesting to read stories of their exploits. I found about half of the ships that were listed.

It made me feel proud to be a part of history, even though I was not with them on the fighting fronts.

When they returned from the battlefront, those sailors had some stories. It was awesome what I saw when I looked into their eyes. Pictures of some horrible, hushed-up thoughts, others voiced their experiences in a very low tone, and some had to be taken to be treated for mental instabilities. Some were so overwhelmed with what they endured that they talked and talked until they were out of breath.

One sailor was being treated for injuries he received during the invasion of Los Negros Island from the *USS Bush* on February 29, 1944. Doctor Johnson, who was in charge of the medical team and looked after the wounded who were cared for by his group, stated in a report, "The corpsmen did their work so extremely well beyond expectations, and when I told them to do something, no questions were asked, and they did their jobs just right."

Women in the Military During World War Two

Women served in three branches of the service. In the army they were the Women's Army Corps Service (WACS), in the navy they were the Women's Acceptance for Volunteer Emergency Services (WAVES), the Coast Guard women were named Semper Paratus – Always Ready (SPARS). Over 86,000 served. Many chose military duty instead of working in defense plants that made war goods.

They had to be between 21 and 44 with no children under the age of fourteen. They also needed special military training. Nurses were brought closer than ever to the front lines. Some were called Grisly Scrub Nurses. Treating the injured was done in some environments that had horrible and awkward conditions in which to work. Over 56,000 nurses served.

Some survivors of Japanese imprisonment acquired Post-Traumatic Stress Disorder (PTSD) when they returned home. Nurses of World War Two got little recognition for their service, but will not be forgotten by military personnel.

From March 20, 1944, and for the following nine months, the hospital ship *USS Solace* treated the injured between New Guinea and the Admiralty Islands. It was capable of caring for up to 450 people at the full height of operations.

I Grew Up With Joe

I called him Billy. His second name was William. His brother told me to only call him Joe because to him, Billy sounded childish, but I continued to call him Billy.

We met at the age of ten. One morning, as I left the rear door of our house, leaning against the building was a strange, 24-inch-wheel bicycle. It had wooden handle bats and a wooden seat bolted over the rear wheel. As I checked if it was rideable, Billy ran from across the street and said, "I am going to your school with my brother, Steve." I called my mom and after questioning them about their home and family, she allowed them to park the bike in our yard during school hours. They lived a mile from us and we remained friends for life.

When the war broke out, without hesitation Billy signed in to the Navy before anyone else in the seventeen-year age group. After boot, he was assigned to the destroyer *USS Callaghan* (DD-792). Even though his ship was in Oakland, California, at the same time I was stationed across the bay in Tanforan, we did not get together before his departure on February 5, 1944.

They plunged right into action with the Fifth Fleet in smashing air raids at Palau, Yap, Ulithi, and Woleal around March 30. Their duties kept them out at sea for eighteen months. The crew rejoiced when they were told they would return to the United Stated. They had one final night of picket duty. Billy was a baker and worked in the galley below.

On July 29, 1944, the ship's alarm sounded and Billy ran topside to assist the gun crew. As soon as he reached the upper deck, a bomb hit the starboard side and penetrated the engine room, which began to sink the ship. The bow bent downward and the fantail stuck up in the air, the props still turning above the water. Billy hollered to those jumping overboard to wait for the props to stop turning, but some were so anxious to leave the aft section of the sinking ship that the blades hit them. They never returned to the surface.

Before getting his life vest completely on when he first got on deck, he was hit in the back with steel shrapnel. He received a gash in his back muscle about six inches by two inches, and one inch deep.

He told me the greatest pain was when he jumped in the salty ocean water and it touched the open wound. A deep scar remains on his back.

The survivors were quickly picked up out of the water by nearby ships. He, with the other injured, received the Purple Heart. It was a quick, short enemy attack.

After the war we liked to swim a lot, often spending many days at the lake. Only once did Billy join us. He felt self-conscious about his ugly scar.

Ignoring the Safety Rules

On September 15, 1944, at about 1:30 p.m., a bombardment of Morotai Island began, three-hundred miles northwest of New Guinea. A stronghold of one-thousand Japanese held and fortified the island. It had to be taken by our military in order to establish an airstrip to further the war effort and defeat the enemy.

The gun crew on one ship – Buddy, George, Charlie, Howard, Hugo, and the gun captain Don, proceeded firing rounds from the gun. During the hasty firing, some ammunition failed to fire. More ammunition was tried, but failed. Old, water-soaked ammo would do that.

Buddy carried the bad ones in his arm, across the open deck to the side of the ship, and threw them overboard. During all the action, and not having much time to stop, look, and think, Buddy walked beneath the gun barrel as it began firing. That was a no-no. He said his heart did not start beating again until he got back to his station at the gun mount. Don and Hugo thought he walked back kind of funny.

Years after at a reunion, they discussed that particular incident. They all agreed that from the time they served, their hearing got bad, their eyes weakened, their bodies twitched in ways they could not control, and their hair turned gray before their senior years.

A Kamikaze Attack

A Japanese suicide pilot carried explosives on his plane, and flew it straight into a ship at sea. The most vulnerable to attack were battleships, aircraft carriers, fuel tankers and ammunition ships.

One sailor who served on the *USS Stevens* revealed a story while he served in the Pacific with Task Force #78 as a gunner on a 5-inch gun.

"We departed from Leyte Gulf in the Philippines, cleared the Surigao Straits and wound up in the Mindanao Sea. Although each ship was armed, most of the convoy's defense fell upon the destroyers.

"Since several situations were spotted on radar, we were all assigned to stand watch at our battle stations. As the ship rolled starboard, I saw the USS Burke, loaded with about 4,000 tons of ammo, sailing low in the water. It became the chosen target of a Japanese kamikaze pilot, who flew his plane right into it. The plane exploded, disintegrating the ship in seconds. It caused a large cloud of smoke and huge waves that bounced smaller vessels sailing in the convoy like they were dancing on water. Even with 28 armed guards on board, they could not stop the plane from getting through the firing line."

A Story by Earl Hickman

It was an assignment I would never forget. It was the Battle of Corregidor. It is a hilly rock island with honey-combed caves connected by tunnels. It was a very important stronghold of the Japanese, protecting the main channel to the Manila harbor area of the Philippines Islands.

A small task force, which consisted of two cruisers and four destroyers, was dispatched to locate and destroy the gun emplacements on shore. With my being on the upper level in the 40-mm gun area, I was able to see all the action taking place.

A single line of eight vessels approached the shore, led by two minesweepers, followed by four destroyers and two cruisers. As they sailed in very slowly, they drew fire from the shoreline, showing positions from the muzzle flashes of the enemy guns. That was the target to fire upon. The eight-inch guns on the two cruisers fired and knocked out the hidden shoreline batteries.

One destroyer hit a mine and the second one, the USS Redford hit a mine while rushing to its aid.

The USS Jenkins stayed aside and waited for the invasion forces to land. Planes carrying fifty paratroopers apiece from the 503rd regiment were released over the hilly side of the island on February 16, 1945, at 8:33 a.m. Eight did not have enough time for their chutes to billow out and open – they bounced on the ground and did not survive. It was a horrible sight.

It was difficult driving the enemy out of those caves. Some of our troops had gasoline tanks strapped to their backs and sprayed the flame into the entrance, and that flushed out the enemy. Some Japanese who hid behind rocks outside the cave would fire at those tanks, causing them to explode, killing the soldier.

Those running out of the caves were engulfed by the burning

gasoline. Many saw it was hopeless to fight any longer and blew themselves up with hand grenades. Some escaped and swam away from the island, only to be killed or drowned to avoid capture. The philosophy of suicide was called, "Bushido."

It was surprising to learn what a large amount of soldiers lives in that hill. Many of those who surrendered were very young and starved for food.

A Non-Active Gun

While operating out of Hollandia, Russ, the gun trainer of their gun, who sat on the right side in the metal seat, waited and waited for something to happen. His butt became paralyzed. Russ was a tall, lanky guy who stood six feet. Earl, the pointer, was short. They both adjusted their seats to fit their body size, mainly for leg comfort.

When one's legs cramped, they switched seats and adjusted them for comfort. They hacked away, telling each other stories.

A Japanese plane came flying in on the starboard side and bore down on them, about 300 feet above the water. It was a Betty – a low-level bomber. There was pandemonium. Russ took a leap for his own seat, but it was adjusted for Earl's short legs. Earl jumped into Russ's seat, adjusted for his long legs. Firing was allowed at will during attacks, but in haste, neither one remembered to unlock the safety. Russ could not move the gun sideways, and as the pointer, Earl could not move the gun up and down to fire in time. Nothing got fired – not a single shot.

As soon as all quieted, the gun captain's response to those

two guys was such that you would not want to hear.

A Scary Situation
Told by my friend

In February, 1944, we were assigned to the battleship task force in the Truk Island area. During one very dark night, the *USS Washington* and the *USS Indiana*, while moving quite fast in the dark, crashed into each other. One of the damaged ships called in to have its ammo removed. We gunner's mates had that job.

As soon as we arrived and began tying to the damaged ship, its bells and sirens blared loudly across the water, indicating general alarm. We were told to untie our boat and shove off, which we did.

We drifted into the dark, away from all the vessels while the ship's guns fired, lighting up the sky all over.

We hunched in our kapok life vests as tightly as ever, expecting the worst to happen out there in "No Man's Waters." The gun firing stopped after a few minutes. We looked around and saw that we had drifted in complete darkness, since most ships were far away. Finally, after some time, one ship scanned its searchlight across the water and found us.

We resumed our duties and were happy to again be attached to something and not drifting in the darkness.

Typhoon Cobra

On the morning of December 18th, 1944, in the wee hours before breakfast, the wind howled viciously through the openings on both sides of our Quonset hut. The temperature dropped to 70 degrees. Too cold for Manus? With that, I knew that with the gusts of wind getting stronger by the minute, it would be a slow-moving work day for me. My thin blanket did not keep me warm, so I got dressed, ran to the mess hall and ate. Many did not get out of their bunks and skipped their meal. No work that day – too windy.

As the day went on, some played cards, wrote letters, or enjoyed a few games of Ping-Pong. The wind grew stronger by the hour.

Our officer in charge came out from his living quarters and said that a raging storm in the Philippines was headed toward the Admiralty Islands. Some wind gusts reached as high as 60 miles per hour. We were advised to fend for ourselves and cope with it the best we could when it arrived.

I looked out to the ocean and saw our boatswain at the dock, working on his 65-foot LCM. He had his head down in the engine compartment, his feet stuck up in the air. The dock and his craft nudged a bit as each ten-foot wave buffeted the structure.

I went with two buddies to go and help the guy. When we got to the water's edge, it was scary. Moisture flooded the air from the ocean, causing poor visibility across the beach front. Those ten-foot-high waves walloped the shore with a crunching sound crashing through crates of eggs, or loud thunder. Some of those wind gusts must've reached 100 miles per hour. It flattened me on the red clay. Then my body lifted up slightly. I was very scared.

We kept our boatswain friend company until his repair job was complete. I asked him, "What was so important that it couldn't wait until the wind ceased?"

He said that the officers relied on him to have the boat available as soon as the storm was over. "They needed to get the ships in the harbor for a special meeting."

Minor damage was seen around Lugos Mission camp after the storm.

Sure enough, the news came out the next day. The storm had been named Typhoon Cobra. It occurred in the Philippine Sea, with wind gusts as high as 140 miles per hour. The storm caused the loss of three destroyers, 146 aircraft, 28 smaller vessels, and 790 lives in Admiral Halsey's 3rd Fleet, Task Force 38.

The war in the Pacific was "on hold." It became a readjustment period for all the strategies planned prior to the typhoon.

One surviving sailor said he looked for some object to knock himself out with because he was scared of the thought of drowning. Some who were badly injured after their ship sunk and were adrift in life rafts allowed themselves to fall into the water and be attacked by the waiting sharks swimming close by.

US President Gerald Ford served on the *USS Monterey* while it was a part of the team in that storm. He slipped on the slippery-wet steel deck but grabbed a stationary section of the vessel just in time, which kept him from going over the side of the ship, which listed back and forth by about 25 degrees.

After Typhoon Cobra subsided, damaged ships arrived at Seeadler Harbor and waited their turn to be repaired.

In my mind, I pictured those sailors, close to 2,000, who were strapped to their bunks below decks on an aircraft carrier. Swaying back and forth must have made them pretty seasick.

At this point, I began to think how so many incidents occurred during my one year gone by in the Navy and all without a serious mishap. I surmised about what the next few weeks would bring – a lot more hard work. Nightmares about danger began to enter my dreams in the middle of the night. My bunk partner Tom awoke from bad dreams and I soothed him at times like a big brother.

My Friend Paul

One morning when I lived in Missouri between 1980 and 2002, there was a letter for me in my post office box that looked like it was jerked out of a jammed paper shredder. The one-man postmaster in Barnett, with a population of 103, said, "Sorry about the condition of your letter, I had no more tape to do a better job."

It was a letter from my friend Paul, a Navy buddy, inviting me to a Lion Four reunion. It was when Betty and I decided to move out of Missouri and relocate to Illinois. We chose Joliet – it turned out to be a good move.

After settling in and adjusting to the new 'everything,' the invitation to the reunion with my Navy friends really bugged me. I caved in; my decision was made and Betty and I went.

The reunion was held at a motel in Clare, Michigan, during September. We signed in a day early in order to get acquainted with the area and do some shopping in town.

The next morning, the day of the reunion, only twenty showed up – Bud and his wife Connie from Ann Arbor, Warner and his wife from Temperance, Ed came from Minnesota, and Paul with Mildred and others from within 200 miles.

As they climbed from their autos, I looked at each one and said to myself, "Those people are old." We hugged, and I said to my buddies, "I haven't seen you guys since 1945 – over sixty years ago!"

Paul and I went gung-ho with our conversation, which

lasted for half an hour. When things cooled down a bit and everyone checked into their rooms, we all walked to a nearby restaurant for lunch. Tables were grouped together for our gang. We spoke about our civilian lives. We Navy guys, with our boisterous voices, were heard throughout the entire room as we told our war stories to each other. It got louder as we ate.

I assumed we had gotten out of hand because, after eating, a man approached our table. He said, "We all listened to your Navy experiences and we want to thank you for your service." Then he quickly grabbed our checks from the table, went to the cashier, and paid for our meals.

In the motel, a conference room was available for us, and there we spent the entire day chatting our heads off. Some brought snacks and Mildred brought apple cider for us to binge on. In the evening, Paul took his guitar out of the case and we all joined in on singalongs with his music. Paul also wrote music and entertained folks at lodges, hospitals, and nursing homes all around Michigan.

I asked Paul where he did Boot. He said, "At Great Lakes, Illinois."

I asked him, "Where do you live?"

"In Sheridan, Michigan."

"How did you get across the lake to enlist?" I asked.

"They had ferries that took people across the lake at that time."

"Where is Sheridan?"

"On Highway 66, slightly west of Holland Lake."

I asked him, "How big is your town?"

"It's so small that on the highway sign, one side says

216

'Entering,' and on the back of the sign it says, 'Leaving.'"

We enjoyed our reunion tremendously. It only lasted one day, but it will remain in my memory forever.

When parting, I took some pictures with others in the lobby of the motel while saying our goodbyes. Then Paul invited me and Betty to their home. The following year we visited them. That is when Paul told me of his experiences on the *USS Jenkins* after transferring from Lion Four.

He started out as a torpedoman with the Lion Four group. He finished his schooling on torpedoes at bases on the west coast of California while I learned about guns.

After that, the first echelon of Lion Four started to form at Tanforan for overseas duty. The torpedomen clicked together separately from the gunner group. We were two separate groups but we always remained buddy-buddy.

Because our work differed, specific duties kept us apart until it was time for recreation, then we joined each other and shared the same equipment and facilities. It was obvious we were as one family. We all lived in the same area in the Lugos Mission camp on the hill, the beautiful ocean below.

One morning our supervisor ordered us to report to the beach for a special announcement. We were told some of us would transfer. Some ships in the harbor needed crew fill-ins. Names were called out and Paul heard his.

A torpedoman was needed on the destroyer *USS Jenkins*. Paul got that job. After the announcements were completed about those transferred, they had to report to their new stations within the hour.

Paul's ship was 376 feet long – a Fletcher-class destroyer which was a popular design. It was equipped with five 5.38-inch guns, ten 20-inch torpedo tubes, six depth-charge projectors, and two depth-charge racks. The ship's top speed was 36 knots and it carried a total of 273 officers and enlisted men.

On the ship, Paul joined a crew of seasoned, battle-worn sailors. They sailed straight to Subic Bay and over to Tarakan Island by Borneo. The ship's crew was told their mission was to destroy the enemy's defense before our invasion troops landed. The island has facilities to refuel ships. It would be an add-on to our defense perimeter.

As they sailed into the battle zone, P-38s were still raiding with gunfire and bombs, with the Australian Navy's assistance. It lasted for hours. When the battle was finished, the *USS Jenkins* was the last to leave the once-Japanese-held area.

"Chow down" was announced over the speakers and everyone headed for the galley. Sandwiches were served and the tables were occupied quickly. All the ships pulled out when all became settled and quiet. What happened next was told to me by Paul with sadness showing on his face.

"While pulling out to open waters, our ship hit a mine. The explosion ripped a hole through the hull at the engine room. The lights went out for a second then the emergency lights lit up the galley. The tables flattened down to the deck. Oil mixed with sea water gushed in from the flooded engine room, through the galley hatchway, and it rose very quickly. We pushed each other to exit through the small galley exit that led to our living quarters. That line moved slowly and I was last in line. I looked around and saw there was no way I would survive as the water was entering so fast, about a foot a minute. Fortunately we got into a room but water kept flooding the ship. Lieutenant Remillard saw the hatches had to be closed to stop the inflow of water causing the ship to sink. He grabbed some diving apparatus and dove way down, closing five open hatch doors, which stopped the flow of water. Everyone kept hollering, 'heads up, heads up,' during those frantic moments. The water was so deep that the short guys were helped by the taller ones to keep them from drowning. I was not a good swimmer, and Paul Weir was my hero for helping me stay afloat."

Someone got to the pumps and emptied the water from the flooded compartments, which stopped the ship from sinking.

We all wound up topside – the injured, the burned, the oil-soaked. The next morning a ship came alongside. It was a cruiser – the *USS Boise* or the *USS Phoenix*. "As soon as I climbed aboard, I washed the oil from my body with the ship's house water." The injured were cared for and all were provided with new clothing from the ship's commissary and fed a good meal.

A discussion began as to why no enemy attacked when the ship was dead in the water, and all the other ships gone.

"As the ship took us to Subic Bay, the sailors treated us very well. When we were sitting in harbor, we saw the damaged *USS Jenkins* pass right by us while in tow, straight to dry dock for repairs."

When resting on deck, a sailor approached and asked for Paul Mahan.

"That's me," he said.

The man handed him his wrist watch, which had his name

on it. He found it while cleaning the Jenkins' galley before repairs started.

Paul told me the wristband of the watch was made from some aluminum scrap taken from a damaged fighter plane, and he asked his buddy to stamp his name on the band. The watch did not work, but what a talking piece it became.

After repairs were completed, the ship sailed out the next day. It pulled out of Subic Bay and headed straight for Pearl Harbor.

On that trip the sea was rough all the way, so everyone strapped to their bunks. I imagined how those 2,000 did the same on aircraft carriers during Typhoon Cobra. Security was maintained on the entire ship, regardless. We were fed from K-rations, which contained spam and crackers.

It was a short, one-day stay at Pearl Harbor, and the final destination was Long Beach, California – the good ole USA. "As I got off the ship, my wildest emotion caused me to kneel down and kiss the ground, as many did."

"On my way home, my mind pictures three small, intriguing worlds I have been to – Tanforan, Manus Island, and Borneo. The best was Home Sweet Home."

Bud

Bud was a real promulgator. He was very convincing while he presented his ideas. One day he talked Sims, our buddy from Alabama, to help him build a diving platform at the edge of the river. Together they constructed it from boards and dunnage left by the Seabees when they first landed. They found enough good lumber to do the job.

They lacked the tools to do a very good job, but figured it was structurally sound. Well, when the word spread that their first dive would be the test, I acted quickly. I ran and got my camera – I was not about to miss that shot.

When they dove and hit that board, it was supposed to spring them in the air and into the water – oh-oh, guess what? They not only showed that they were poor carpenters, but also the jolt on the board attached to the platform made it collapse, and they both fell to the ground. We all ran to their aid. They ignored help from our pharmacist, and with good reason. Why? Their structure was not an approved recreation facility, so therefore injuries would be noted in their personnel file as being a misdemeanor. So for the next few days, Bud and Sims could not hide their limping and bruises.

There were only three places to entertain ourselves – on the small ball field, in the rec hut to play ping-pong, or down at the beach below the hill, a few hundred yards from our campsite. Swimming was my personal pleasure. Bud almost always joined me down there. Our officers never disturbed us when we were at play; they always stayed away from us. They knew how hard and diligently we worked, so they respected our time off.

At times when Bud and I were down at the beach – uh-oh – marines came in for beach-landing practice. Only one thought entered my mind – vamoose! Straight up the hill I ran, as quickly as possible to get away. Boat after boat dumped those rifle-ready marines onto the shore as they ran wildly, firing their weapons into the thick, desolate jungle. It was their mock invasion. They practiced for six hours then returned to their ships in the harbor. By morning, I saw that their ships and some others were gone.

A Horrible Event

I feel strongly compelled to relate this story of the tragic event that occurred during the night of July 30th, 1945, right smack in the deep waters of the Pacific Ocean. It bears heavily on my mind to this day.

As the war went into its fourth year, stories of many terrible tragedies spread amongst the sailors in the Pacific. One story continued to top the last one, and I thought we were close to the end of the war. There was still danger lurking all about, and in the dark. This story is about a ship sinking and shark attacks. The ship was the cruiser *USS Indianapolis* (CA-35).

We on Manus received the information soon after the survivors were rescued from the sunken ship. When hearing of it, I could not fathom the horrible, chilling information as it crept so deeply into my mind.

The ship was over 600 feet long, its top speed was 32 knots per hour, it held over 1,000 men and could travel over 10,000 miles on a mission.

After some minor repairs, it proceeded to Tinian Island with about half the world's uranium (U-235) at the time. It was for Little Boy, the bomb that would later be dropped on Hiroshima. After the Indianapolis raced with its bomb cargo from San Francisco to Pearl Harbor then Tinian, it went to Guam for some crew replacements. It left on the 28th and sailed for Leyte to train crew members. From there it left to Okinawa to join Task Force 95. At 14 minutes after midnight, on July 30th, she was struck on her starboard bow by two Type-95 torpedoes from the Japanese submarine I-58 under the command of Motochitsura Hashimoto.

The explosion caused massive damage, The Indianapolis listed heavily and settled by the bow. Twelve minutes later she rolled over completely, her stern rising in the air, then she plunged straight down.

Some 300 of the 1,196 men on board went down with the ship. With few lifeboats launched, many sailors without life jackets were set adrift into the dark of night.

Navy command had no knowledge of the ship's sinking until three days later on August 2nd, at 10:25 a.m., when the patrol plane Ventura (PV-1), flown by Lt. Chuck Gwinn and co-pilot Lt. Warren Colwell, on a routine flight, spotted the men adrift. All air and surface units capable of rescue were dispatched to the scene at once. The men in the rafts and in the water suffered from lack of food and water. They found some rations such as spam and crackers amongst the floating debris. Soon, other problems surfaced for those on the rafts and in the water. Hypothermia – exposure to the cold, dehydration – not enough drinking water, desquamation – lack of body salt, photophobia and dementia.

One can only imagine what that was like. The Pacific Ocean is a huge body of water. Because ships were large and heavy, they could not get to a disaster scene quickly. Some survivors soon died from the severe conditions. Some killed themselves because they were so exhausted and their minds groped with unclear thoughts.

After all the information was collected on that tragedy, some said that the ship's sinking resulted in the most shark attacks known in history.

A Catalina seaplane commanded by Lt. Marks went to lend assistance. He also flew over the *USS Cecil J. Doyle* and alerted its captain, who then diverted from his route to assist. Marks' crew got there first and dropped rubber rafts and supplies to the survivors in the water. The lone swimmers were at greatest risk of shark attacks and were pulled out first. When Marks' plane was full, men were tied to the wings with parachute cords and brought to safety. Captain Clayton turned his powerful searchlight into the night and found drifters in the water, disregarding his own safety and possible attack by the enemy. Marks and his men rescued 56 men that day.

The destroyers *Helm, Madison*, and *Ralph Talbot* were ordered to the rescue scene from Ulithi. The destroyer escorts *Dufilho, Bassett*, and *Ringness* left from the Philippines Sea and assisted in the rescue.

After the war, there was controversy at a court martial hearing to find out why the commander of the Indianapolis did not zig-zag in unsecured waters. The Japanese sub commander said it would have made no difference.

That tragedy scared me into thinking I would be transferred to a front-line ship. I assumed I had a little more experience than some of my buddies and that was what officers chose to have under their command.

A shortage of physically fit single men on the civilian front began to show. Some limitations at induction centers were adjusted and more men were taken into the military. Many of us talked about the war ending soon, but they began inducting married men that had two children. When would it all end?

One man I knew back home who worked in an aircraft factory wrote in the mail to me, "For heaven's sake, get that war over with."

When the war finally did end and I returned home, a different person said to me, "Why did you guys have to end the war so soon? I made lots of money in the defense factory."

He was not my friend.

Mandrin Island

O nly a few days had gone by since the Indianapolis had sunk. Ships of all types entered the harbor. Some came for small-caliber ammunition and others to remove unwanted explosives. It was a quiet scene for a few days. An Australian corvette – a ship that was a good sub-chaser and minesweeper – the size of our Navy's destroyer escort, sailed into the harbor like a lady on parade for an anchor spot. She entered not with a toot-toot of the ship's horn but a loud-as-ever baw-baw-baw at about 8 a.m., heard for miles.

At 9 a.m., Lt. "B" came into our living quarters and asked for Hoppy and me. He assigned the two of us to deliver bombs to Mandrin Island and then stand watch there for a few days. We were given a .45-caliber Colt automatic pistol and a .30-caliber Mk. 1 carbine rifle with a bag full of mixed cartridges for both weapons that weighed about thirty pounds.

We went down to the beach where the LCM was already loaded with 250-pound bombs, and the boatswain was waiting for us to board. A small crane was with the load. The 65-foot-long boat was a much-used one that showed its wear and tear, with wrinkles on both sides in many places. So heavy was our load that the LCM looked to be at a sinkable point. With the ramp closed, the engines revved up so loud that it sounded like two bears growling in a tunnel at the top of their voices. The boat freed from the ground, turned around, and headed straight for Mandrin Island, which was about nine miles northeast of Manus Island.

Hoppy and I sat on the gunwale of the boat as we sailed, and wondered how it stayed afloat with that weight. The steel sides had slight cracks which opened and closed while bouncing over each wave. I was prepared for any possible sinking as we sailed on that short, forty-minute trip.

The boatswain saw us looking at those cracks but he just motioned for us to not worry about it.

On Mandrin Island, the eastern shoreline was the only possible landing. The waves were about thirty inches high. When the boat ramp was dropped on the shore, it steadied the boat, which was good. We carried the two coolers in the shade next to a coconut tree. One contained sandwiches, the other had drinking water. The one carbine rifle was loaded and set next to a cooler.

The island is only about three city blocks long, three-fourths of a city block wide, half of it shaded by coconut trees and the other half covered with thick brush as high as five feet. The highest point of the island was only four or five feet above sea level.

The three of us unloaded the bombs and stacked them in a pile, under the shade of the coconut trees. When the boat was empty, it posed a problem for the boat driver. He struggled with the controls to avoid hitting the coral reefs as the boat bounced up and down on those wild waves. He finally succeeded and we waved him off as he headed back to Manus Island. The first thing we did was check our weapons. Armed with our rifle and pistol, we walked along the shore, observing what was on the island. I had my shoes off and walked on the shoreline, sifting sand and water with my bare feet. I felt at ease enjoying the beauty of the bright, blue sky and the ocean.

Then I felt what I thought was a wooden stick floating in the water, and the tip of it hit my ankle… but it was not a stick. I looked down and saw that it was a deadly, twelve-inch long coral snake. No one ever lived longer than one hour if bitten by one. It frightened me so much that when I saw it, I became petrified with such fear; my body felt ashen and cold, even in the 110-degree heat. Another look showed me that the snake was dead. I then assumed some native killed it and threw it in the water. I was so relieved.

Hoppy and I walked around that entire island in about 25 minutes. Then we discussed the fact that we were very vulnerable to unknown dangers. We had no backup protection, so I said to Hoppy, "Let's just do our job and not worry."

At about noon, a native outrigger sailed close to shore and anchored near the underwater coral beds. With their hand-carved wooden spears, they took turns and dove to spear some fish. They dropped about ten fish into their boat and they all swam to shore. A young one climbed a coconut tree and dropped three coconuts to the ground. Then, with the same fishing spear, he shucked all three and in one he poked a hole and drank milk from it. He did not care for the mean and offered it to us. I saw one wore goggles he used for diving that were carved out of a gas mask found in the litter of the Manus Island invasion. I asked them to pose for a photograph, which they did after I showed them my camera. Heavy waves started bouncing their outrigger so they waved to us and sailed away.

Evening arrived, we finished eating, and I said, "Let's walk." It was near sundown and as we neared the south side of the island,

229

a single native canoe set on the shore immediately caught our attention. We began to investigate. A male native ran out from the thick brush, waving his arms for us to not enter the brush from which he ran out. He gave us funny hand signals we did not fully understand. My first thought was how do we handle this situation? After a few seconds, Hoppy caught on to what it was all about. The native man's lady was delivering her baby in the brush. Together, all three of us when Hoppy and I finally got the message. The two of us walked away as the native went back into the brush. Hoppy and I moved away but not too far. We thought they would possibly need some help, so we only walked a few hundred feet away and lingered along the shoreline, out of sight.

After forty-five minutes, we heard the cry of a newborn. We waited another half hour and then returned to the site. No one was there. We looked around everywhere and checked everything in the area, but no evidence of any activity in the bush, and the canoe was gone.

The next day was very hot. Hoppy complained a lot. I suggested we take a swim on the west shore where the water was very still and deep. I dove down and explored a cavern. It was the home for a lot of fish, most small ones. I was drawn to explore. In the pit, five feet down, a shelf of coral jutted outward horizontally. Beneath it, at the bottom, I saw the flat coral surface. When I dove in that twenty by twenty by twenty-five foot pit, a bunch of small fish swarmed around me as if I was their next meal, or as if they were plain curious, but they did not even touch me. I could've grabbed any one of them. Two starfish caught my eye down at the bottom. They both had sparkling colors, as beautiful as ever. One was orange, the other a bluish-green. I had to get them. I made a dive, and as I passed fifteen feet, the water pressure made such loud noises in my ears it sounded as if a heavy hammer pounded on my head. I was determined to swim down and get those two brightly colored starfish and bring them to the surface. I dove to the bottom. When I grabbed the two starfish, my head felt like it would burst into two pieces from the water pressure. I laid them on the coral in the blazing hot sun. In less than ten minutes they both died and turned an ugly gray color.

The third day it was also very hot. I looked at the three piles of bombs. I gazed up at the beautiful blue sky, my eyes scanning the rolling waves hitting the white, sandy shore, and not a plane in the sky.

I wondered, "Why did we store all of these bombs since they were constantly needed for the continuing invasions of enemy-held islands? No airplanes in the sky, no boats running around in the harbor, everything as still and quiet as ever as we waited for transportation back to Manus Island.

Hoppy complained some more, reciting the same old stuff. "I didn't join the Navy to do this kind of work." Then he remained quiet until we left the island.

The evening after we returned from the island, someone asked me, "What did you do to Hoppy on Mandrin Island?"

I asked, "What do you mean?"

They all said he's in the booby hatch; Ward 9. He's going home. Hoppy was the same guy who found maggots in his oatmeal at breakfast a while back and ran out of the chow hall.

231

Now rumors floated in the air — we called those "scuttlebutt." Mostly unreliable rumors – or were they? They were about the war ending very soon.

Bud came to me and said, "Let's go down to the river." As we walked, a soldier followed behind us, walking back to his camp across the river. Behind him, a young native boy about ten years old followed him. The boy kept begging the soldier for the small mirror that partially stuck out of his backpack. Most of the military people had one for shaving. He kept telling the boy to scram, but the boy did not go away; he kept following him.

When they both arrived at the river's edge, the soldier had to cross but couldn't because the water was too deep. The boy pointed to the mirror in the backpack and motioned to him again that he wanted it, and if he got it, he would show the soldier where the river was shallow enough to cross. I thought the soldier was not able to swim, so the boy won and got his mirror. I watched the soldier cross with fear.

Bud and Me

Bud hardly ever missed a football game played at the University of Michigan in Ann Arbor. It was his favorite sport. He lived only three streets from there. No parking problem – he walked to the games, rain, snow, or shine. He met his wife Connie there when she performed as a cheerleader at every game.

When I met Bud, it was at Tanforan. We all wanted to be friends and Bud, while we talked, noted that football was his passion. He told us that his uncle was the naval officer that directed his induction ceremony at Great Lakes Naval Academy. As we talked about our training for overseas, he pointed out to me the proper approach toward a suspected enemy in the bush. "Step to the ground with toes like a cat; not with the heels."

"Where did you learn that?" I asked.

He said, "I'm part Indian. Look and see – no hair on my chest, I seldom need a haircut, and you will never see me shave." I forgot what tribe his ancestors were, but his face did show some Indian likeness.

He asked me what my favorite sport was, and I told him swimming. After that, we did the Merchant Marine exercises, he taught me my first high dive during advanced training, and now as we were together on Manus, he invited me to join him in ocean swims at the beach below the hill of the Lugos Mission camp.

It was coincidence that we were both without a work

assignment on that one day. We did not have many opportunities for us to both get down there for a swim. The rough part was always climbing the hill back to camp.

On one very hot, sunny afternoon, Bud said, "We should take a long swim out into the harbor." Without anything to do, I agreed and we both ran down to the beach where the river flowed to the ocean.

He said, "See that lovely cargo ship out there, about a half-mile away? Let's swim to it."

Seeing that the water was very calm in the harbor and the water temperature was pleasant, we took off without a second thought. I never thought about how long it would take to reach the ship or the dangers in the water.

I did a slow dog paddle, and my favorite side stroke, which never tired me after I got my second wind. We took many rests by floating on our backs. It was very leisurely. After half an hour, some small fish pecked on my legs and Bud's as well after a few seconds. It caused me a slight concern.

Once we had swam more than halfway to the ship, we entered larger waves. We then decided to turn around and go back to shore. We had already been in the water for two hours. When we turned back toward the shore, we faced the bright sun to the west. As we neared the shore, my tongue dried, the salt from the water swelled my lips, and my conversation with Bud became unclear.

The swim had been very good so far, but as we approached shore, we had drifted and wound up south of our starting point by about two miles. Then, we encountered three cross-currents. We had to fight them to get to the beach. When I entered the first one, the water just took me back out to my entry point. No forward gain.

With a slightly exhausted voice, Bud said, "You have to fight those currents." I struggled through the first one and thought the second one would be the same struggle, but it was tougher. The third was even more difficult. The current pushed my body back toward deeper water

Bud hollered over the noisy waves as he stood on shore, "Fight as hard as you can!" With that message, I swam as vigorously as I ever did and almost gave up, which would've put me back in deeper water as the tide began to go out to sea. I struggled, and only made it to shore by using all of my strength. We walked the shore for about two miles, then climbed that hill back to our camp.

Days passed quickly as we worked, continually moving ammunition from here to there and back again. From our hut, Bud and I watched a very heavy rainfall, seeing the red clay wash down the hill and into the ocean. When the rain stopped, four or five waves formed in the shape of a cobra snake, ready to strike. The waves were about twenty feet high. I named them "cobra waves."

Bud said, "You should try diving into one of those; it's really fun. I'll show you how the next time it rains hard." That statement left my mind until a few weeks passed. Then Bud came running to me.

"It's raining hard, be ready. We're going to dive those big waves when the rain stops."

When the rain slowed, we slid down the muddy hill and got to the beach just as the first huge wave started rolling in. He said

235

to me, "There will be only four or five big ones, so I will dive into the first one and you will have to dive in the big one right after me before they flatten out."

He dove right beneath the chin of the cobra's head and in a second he disappeared. Then his head popped above the water surface a hundred feet or more away and he swan back to shore with a wave. He hurriedly coaxed me into it. "You can do it. Just dive in, count five seconds, and swim straight up from a twenty-foot depth of water."

I dove in and it was very fast, believe me. I saw with my open eyes how fast I got to that twenty-foot depth, like being fired from a slingshot or being flushed down a toilet or sliding through a tube at a water park. Would that be called an undertow?

The next day we found long, wooden planks to surf on with incoming waves.

Bud's Bad Trip to Mandrin Island

On the evening of April 6th, 1945, the last meal was served and as I meandered back to my Quonset hut, I wondered why Bud and his working party had not returned from Mandrin Island. The work they had with their bombs would not take all day – only a couple of hours and it was only a twenty-five-minute trip back to Manus Island. We were all concerned as we discussed it.

I heard the engines of an LCM down at the beach. It took off after unloading Bud's working party. I walked over to meet Bud and the few members of his crew to learn of his late return from Mandrin Island.

He was the first to approach me. I saw his eyes were bulged out, with this horrible look on his face.

I asked, "What happened?"

The first words out of his mouth were in a very exhausted tone. "We could have used your help. I will tell you about it later."

Earlier that day, Lt. Commander Cunnean and Ensign C. C. Mansur examined the weather and discussed the day's work. Mansur said, "I can probably finish the job today."

At about 10 a.m., Bud and the crew, including Mansur, Best, Bridge, Potter and Orndoff, left Lugos Mission for Mandrin Island with sandwiches and drinks. When the boatswain got close to the island, he was leery of the coral reefs along that deep-water shoreline. There was no other place to beach the boat, and hitting the coral would damage the propellers, disabling the craft. He quickly pulled close to drop off the two men with the food and drinks.

The high waves told him to not try and land the craft on the beach. The men were asked to swim to shore, which was about 75 yards away. Bud jumped in first, thinking they all could swim that distance, and the rest followed as the LCM left.

As they were about halfway to the beach, two men in the water started yelling for help, and further away, two more were in trouble. Bud swam back out to help one get to shore. Ensign Mansur also swam out to help a struggling crew member, but they both went under. Best grabbed a log on the beach and quickly got Bridge, pushing him to shore. Bud, being so exhausted, could not move anymore. The men who perished were Potter and Orndoff, along with Ensign Mansur.

The next morning, divers were sent to the island but found very little evidence of the drowned in the water.

The following day, a court martial was held, and because Bud had the highest rank of the survivors, he took the rap.

Years later, Bud sent me a hand-written letter that explained the situation, and added, "I just wish I could've done more."

Le Shima

Some called it the Peanut Island because of its shape. It's a part of the Ryuku Island group, located slightly east of Okinawa. Because this tiny island was the site of events holding great importance to me, I felt this story must be told.

On April 16th, 1945, the army's 77th Infantry division landed on Shima. It was warfare at its worst. Japanese leaders made it public that they would fight to the bitter end. Not one Japanese soldier would surrender – he would kill or be killed.

There was one outstanding war correspondent who not only followed but actually joined with them in the army's infantry fighting fronts. His pictures and war information were accurate and up-to-date. Back home, folks could hardly wait to see the newsreels across the country that showed his photos and gave his stories firsthand. First in Europe, then in the Pacific.

He was loved by his coworkers, generals, and GIs alike. Friends of his said he was a household name during World War Two. He wrote stories that got right to the heart of the people back home. HE wanted the people to see and understand the sacrifices soldiers had to make in an actual battlefield, fighting the enemy from foxholes. This Indiana farm boy was Ernie Pyle.

On his third day on Le Shima, he and three officers in a jeep came under fire. They all scrambled and took cover in the ditches. When Pyle raised his head, he was killed instantly by a bullet.

A man named Roberts, with other photographers, were at a

command post 300 yards away. Roberts crawled through mud and enemy fire, and recorded with his speed graphic camera what was there.

This was the only photo taken of his death. Because this photo would have an effect on those close to him, it would not surface for many years.

The fighting began on March 25th and lasted for three weeks. The island only had a circumference of twelve miles. The Japanese destroyed part of the airfield. After our troops invaded, the airfield was quickly repaired.

On August 6th, 1945, the United States detonated an atomic bomb on the city of Hiroshima at 8:15 a.m. local time. President Harry S Truman again called for Japan's surrender, warning them, "Expect a rain of ruin from the air, the likes of which has never been seen on this earth."

On August 9th, 1945, the second atomic bomb was dropped on Nagasaki. Hirohito directed his Supreme Council to accepted terms to end the war. On August 15th, 1945, he publicly announced the surrender of Japan to the allies.

Le Shima was a stop-off point for Japanese Lt. Torasirou Kawabe and staff to transfer to a U.S. C-54 plane that took them to Manila. There, they met with General MacArthur and arranged the signing of the peace treaty that took place on the deck of the *USS Missouri* on September 2nd, 1945.

"BETTY" The bomber

JAPANESE DELEGATES

Before the delegates flew to Le Shima, they insisted their planes be marked with green crosses on their wings and body, rather than round, red zeroes.

On the USS Missouri, September 2, 1945, was held the signing of the peace treaty.

The End of World War Two

O n Manus Island, we found out about the Japanese surrender on the 14th, but in the United States it was the 15th because of the different time zones.

If the Japanese had not surrendered, hundreds of troop-filled vessels sitting outside of Tokyo Bay were ready to invade Japan.

With the announcement of the war's end, that evening as the dark closed in, the ship crews celebrated with fireworks. Pyrotechnics lit up the sky in all directions. Some ships fired tracers from their guns. It continued through the night in Seeadler Harbor. It was the largest fireworks display I had ever seen.

Victory in Europe was named, "V-E Day, and victory over Japan was named "V-J Day." People at Pearl Harbor celebrated with enormous vigor on V-J Day. A total of 254 ships gathered in Tokyo Bay on September 2nd, 1945, to witness the surrender signing ceremony.

The following day, a meeting of our officers took place in our camp and we were given information about those going home. I, being in the V-6 program (victory plus six months), was not eligible to leave Manus and remained there for the rest of the program.

The enlistees with contracts of four- or six-year terms had to complete that time. They were transferred from Manus to new assignments elsewhere.

As I faced six more months, I assumed it would be even

longer, seeing all of that mixed ammunition needing to be sorted and stored, and with fewer men to help. I saw more work ahead. A bit despondent, I wrote home and said I may never come back. A very quick letter from my brother scolded me vehemently. "Don't you ever send information like that home again." I then sent home a very soft and smooth letter, which worked out well as I later found out

I was twenty years old.

Ships unloaded ammunition rapidly, then loaded with troops who were homebound. The operation was fast. We called it, "The Magic Carpet."

The Quonset huts provided us a good homestead on the hill. More games of ping-pong were played and I, being the driver of one personnel carrier, was asked to drive men to movies that were shown occasionally at the main base theater located at Lorengau, down the beach about three miles.

Many facilities remained for the native residents all over the Admiralty Islands. The litter left by the military was a gold mine, as it became a product of value to them.

The natives had trails throughout the jungle, leading to their favorite sites. Constant growth over these paths was a menace. The men always led the family packs, swatting wild growth with a machete.

Deep bomb craters that were never filled in became a haven for mosquitoes. Malaria was a constant threat. The natives were paid one dollar per day to spray diesel fuel on the water in those rain-filled holes. Rodents also multiplied in some areas, so certain men brought an eight-foot-tall, galvanized container with a screened cover. When some mice were caught, they were placed in there to be checked for disease. I could not believe the speed and agility mice had when attempting to escape from the container. They zipped up to the top with lightning speed, hit the screen and bounced back to the bottom of the container.

Our pharmacist usually gave us information he received on such health matters, as they were constantly monitored.

It was also time to get rid of unwanted explosives, mostly rounds of ammunition. We loaded one day and dumped the following day. Men of the third and fourth echelons, having been with our Lion Four group a couple of months, already had plenty of experience in handling the heaviest projectiles.

The torpedomen had the same routine, eliminating unwanted equipment and torpedo parts. Lots of their tools, gyros, wiring and accessories got dumped in the ocean.

Shifts were arranged so equal hours suited both shifts. A 65-foot LCM was sent from the boat pool for our use loading and dumping ammunition out in the ocean. The driver of the boat was the one who determined a full load. Our loads consisted of projectiles, pyrotechnics, hedgehogs, rockets, casings of black powder, and many depth-charge boosters.

After moving off the beach with our load, we headed straight out toward open sea. At the moment we lost sight of land over the horizon, we knew it was far enough out to dump – ten to twelve miles offshore.

On one trip, as we neared the dump area, the boat was still moving and we began to throw the smaller items over first. For some reason, when Spoony threw one small, ten-pound depth

245

charge over the side, it exploded beneath the boat, raising it slightly but not damaging it. Someone had overlooked the fuse in it.

In between the days we dumped, we played baseball or went swimming. Many rainfalls hampered our activities. Our commander, Jones, at the age of fifty-five, joined in our baseball games. He was one of those officers who saw how we labored in our duties. "Anyone needing a job after the war, come and see me. I will hire any one of you," was often his reminder. In civilian life, he was a superintendent at a utility and power company in Tennessee.

On another dumping trip, and LCM came to us for loading. It must have been removed from the scrap pile three times, it was in terrible shape from so much use. It vibrated like the sound of beating drums, but both engines ran very smoothly.

We loaded it pretty heavy but the boatswain made no remark about that. As soon as we reached the larger waves, cracks in the steel sides buckled back and forth as the boat raised on each wave. Bates and I watched that happen and we glanced at each other with concerned looks.

At about eight miles out, short of the dump area, Spoony hollered out, "Smoke coming from the ammunition pile!"

The driver immediately shut down both engines. He looked as concerned as we all did, and instantly everything was thrown overboard with the greatest speed. The smoke rose for at least three minutes. It took us about fifty minutes to unload entirely. Then we found the heavy cable lying beneath the deck that powered the ramp in front. It was frayed, causing it to ground against the metal and smoke. There were no powder spills. If there was, it could've been a disaster.

Bates passed out from exhaustion for a minute. We all rested with ever-dry throats, then we all drank two Cokes with the greatest enjoyment.

August14, 1945,
Lugos Mission on Manus Island of the Admiralties.

From left to right, Lenny K., and Nellie.

From left to right, Bud Tracy, Bill Carson, Nellie, Campbell and Powers.

The chapel on the main base at Loregau of Manus Island.

A mushroom cloud from the nuclear explosion over Nagasaki, Japan, rising 60,000 feet in the air on the morning of August 9, 1945.

I left Manus Island on December 23, 1945. Twenty days later This picture was taken right at the age of 21.

Betty Grable was "IT," no two ways about it. Her beautiful legs were insured for one-million dollars. As an actress, she earned $300,000 per year. The Treasury Department reported she was the highest-paid woman in America in 1946 and 1947.

Jane Russell was also a popular pin-up girl. She was a model, an actress, singer and dancer during World War 2. She was born in Bemidji, Minnesota. In 1955 she formed the International Adoption Fund.

Dorothy Lamour was also admired by the troops. Her famous role in the movies was "The Road to Singapore," played with Bob Hope.

Carmen Miranda was the lively one. She danced to Latin music played by Xavier Cugat's band. She was named the "chica-chica-chica-boom chick" girl who always dressed is glorious attire. She was born in Brazil.

The USO

The United Service Organization (USO) was formed by men and women who committed themselves to entertaining the troops away from home. USO centers were located in almost every city across the country during World War Two. I remember that Chicago was the best-liked by the servicemen. Donations to support their activities came from various sources.

A the centers, servicemen were able to meet others in the military. Snacks were serves and dancing went on in many centers. It was a place to relax and also get assistance with various matters.

Some USO members also entertained overseas. Those people encounter some hardships – it was a real sacrifice. They were required to pass a physical test, including inoculations against diseases that were prevalent in the areas they entertained. Singers, dancers, and comedians from Hollywood were the best.

I had not seen any live entertainment during my year on Manus. We all talked a lot about that, and then our officer told us that as soon as the Seabees completed their construction of the theater at Lorengau, some entertainment would arrive.

Some from our Lion Four group went to investigate the progress of the theater. They returned and said, "You will not believe what a large theater those guys built." All the seats were made from chopped-down trees and each log had adze-flattened surfaces for seating. When I saw what was there, I bonked out.

The one show I attended had Bob Hope and his group. It

rained slightly but the show went on. It could not deter hundreds from attending.

Bob was opener onstage, with Martha Raye, different in her comedy style, Tony Romano strumming his guitar, and Jerry Colona with his jokes.

Frances Langford sang and danced, then asked for men in the audience to stand up and identify which state they lived in. When she asked for anybody from Texas, many stood up. Pearson, who was from Texas, did not get up, so we prompted him a bit roughly. Frances saw our commotion from the stage and hollered, "Who is that shy guy from Texas? Send him up here pronto."

We heaved him up there pronto. Then Frances said, "I know you. You are one of my neighbors."

The entire audience immediately got as quiet as ever to hear what was next. Frances said, "Your buddy should be entertaining with us because he plays the violin like a professional." After a bit of encouragement, he was handed a violin and played, accompanied by the band. They made some beautiful music. We never knew he was talented.

The show was very entertaining, even while sitting on the hard logs all that time.

The show started at 8 p.m. and ended at 10 p.m. Then the huge crowd dispersed, flowing in all directions. Many got in their jeeps and went back to their camps on Manus and Los Negros, but most were from ships in the harbor and they headed for the dock for a boat to take them back.

Because Lugos Mission camp was kind of an isolated area, about two miles from the theater, there were no roads inland from the ocean. We had to go back the same way we went there – along the shoreline.

I was the driver who had to drive back the eight I brought to the theater. With the one heavy downpour and continuing rain throughout the show, puddles got larger in the red, slippery clay road back to camp. The clouds were gone, the moon as bright as ever. Headlights did no good. As I drove, it was puddle after puddle, some deep and some not. Because there were no washroom facilities at the theater, the guys hollered to drive faster. When I hit deep puddles, they almost threw men out of the vehicle. However, we made it back.

	IRVING BERLIN	
SECTION	---AND--- THE ORIGINAL CAST IN	DAY
B	"This Is The Army"	4
	NAVAL BASE THEATER	

Martha Raye, Frances Langford, Bob Hope, Jerry Colona

The following days, the same thing – work and rest. We used our spare time between jobs, crafting objects from scraps found in dumps left in certain areas. We made some souvenirs and sent them home. I made a few candleholders from small cartridge casings and a few hula skirts out of parachute flare cords colored with dye. I found small pieces of Lucite and made a picture frame by bending a shape in boiling water on a small fire. Mercurochrome was added to the water, which made the Lucite pink.

Hocker, who was from Wisconsin, experimented with Cosmoline, and since Lucite and Plexiglas came about, he said, "When I get home I am going to build boats made of fiberglass."

Another buddy in our hut was always sketching figures of women's garments on scrap pieces of paper. He wanted to start a clothing business of his own when he was discharged. Two others studied lessons they received from the International Correspondence School they signed up with.

A few took their allowed leave time and sailed to Australia, including Carson and Barney. When they returned after two weeks, Carson had an emergency appendectomy and was told to take it easy. He did not because he felt guilty, seeing others lifting those 5.38-inch projectiles. He joined them, and wound up in the hospital for a few days.

The violinist who played on stage had an accident. A few weeks after the entertainment at the Lorengau theater, he and two other guys experimented with the construction of a small moonshine still far back in the jungle during their days off work. An overabundance of raisins were available to us at meals but many did not care to eat the rice pudding made with them. Those three set out with the objective of making a drink called Raisin Jack. Late one afternoon I heard an explosion. The still blew up and all three were badly burned. Later in the evening, I heard all three died.

Belirma and Pomumu

Three of us, Benjy, Perry and I, decided to explore and see what was up along Liheli River. Perry took a carbine rifle and I took a pistol. We all had our hip knives.

We walked up the river for ten minutes, so far that the ocean was out of sight. A small, rickety canoe lay on a narrow part of the river bank. I got in and as I paddled, dangling my feet in the water, an elderly native saw me and motioned a "no-no" sign for me leaving my legs in the water. In broken English and sign language he explained those small, squat, four-inch-ling fish swirling around my feet would eat my flesh to the bone in a few minutes if I was bruised. After a few minutes of jibber-jabbering, I surely got the message. I had no reason to doubt his word, and pulled my feet out of the water.

A lagoon veered out from the river's edge and caught my eye. Benjy and I paddled with our hands to that small, perfectly still, lagoon. Mocha-colored sand swirled with the water, sparkling around the canoe. My thought was, "quicksand." It appeared only inches deep. I put my legs in the water and felt no bottom. I got frightened and pulled my legs back into the canoe, then we moved back up the river quickly. The water got very shallow so we shored the canoe and proceeded along the river bank on foot.

A small, injured crocodile was in the mud, barely alive. It looked like someone tried to kill it with a machete. I fired my pistol twice to end its suffering.

The day was very hot; no breeze at all, so we headed back to the mouth of the river near the ocean. At about 2 p.m., we got company. Two native boys popped out of the jungle like magic. I figured they wanted something, but what? I asked them their names. One said Belirma and the other said Pomumu. We rested on a log in the shade near a wide, flat area and talked together.

Some very tall eucalyptus trees grew close by. On the upper tree branches, fruit bats hung by their wing claws, asleep. Al night long they flew around, devouring mosquitoes for food.

Belirma, the younger boy, pointed to Perry's carbine rifle, and motioned for him to shoot a bat up in the tree (the bat is food for the natives). Perry grew up with a rifle, and was a rabbit-hunter in the Carolinas. He answered Belirma with his best sign language that the bats were too far away and he would only hit one in the wing and injure it.

The two boys understood and ran back into the jungle, out of sight. As we sat in the shade and joked, suddenly Belirma and Pomumu came out of the bushes with a dead, 24-inch-long snake, and plopped it on the large, sandy ground. Pomumu motioned with his hands to wait. He kept pointing at the bats in the trees, Perry's rifle, and the snake on the ground. We got their message, but were not convinced that the bats would come for the snake. Bats didn't fly in the daylight.

The boys were correct. After twenty-five minutes, bat after bat, all sizes large and small, dove for the snake. Perry, the sharpshooter, took aim as the bats paused to grip the dead snake. It posed a perfect target for Perry and he got those bats one after another.

256

We felt the wings. They were very thin and rubbery, like an innertube, and with very silky, smooth skin.

What woke up the bats? As the snake swelled in the very hot sun, it fermented, which caused some strong scents to reach their senses, signaling them that food was nearby. It had to be strong to alert them.

The largest bat's body weighed about three pounds. After we posed for a picture, the two native boys, Belirma and Pomumu, picked up the bats, and with a smile waved goodbye to us.

After all that we plunged into the ocean, swam for a while, then trudged up that long, steep hill and straight for the chow hall for our evening meal.

Work, Play, and Wait

Waiting was the dominant thought on my mind. Once the war ended, the attitude of all the officers and enlisted men seemed a bit relaxed. I had to wait a couple more months before getting a ticket home. Lots of letter-writing. I had only a few people to write to: My parents, my three brothers, and a couple of girls I knew from high school. The girls stopped writing me as soon as I went overseas. I cannot even remember their names.

It was clear what our daily work would be for the remainder of our stay on Manus Island. I routinely drove a crew of men to some work site that required storing projectiles no longer needed on ships. Some boats were loaded with explosives to be dumped in the ocean. Between jobs, I also cut hair for a lot of people in the corner of the recreation hut.

Three of us usually hung together in the evenings. We sat outside our Quonset hut and drank our bottle of Michelob when they were passed out. When we got a bottle at the chow hall, they punched a hole in our beer chit, limiting us to one bottle per person The bottle caps got rusted during the long voyage across the ocean.

During our usual get-together at sundown, the air around us suddenly filled with half-inch flying ants that came out from the base of some nearby palm trees. The large, thick, black swarm attacked us and tried to get into our eyes, ears, nose and mouth. None bit us, but their menacing attack lasted for about two minutes before the sky cleared.

One night I laid against the tree with Stovepipe. We gazed at the sky and remarked how beautiful it was, so full with stars. The Big Dipper was upside-down, versus right-side up at home (north of the Equator). He said to me, "Look out in the harbor at those guys on the deck of that ship watching a movie."

I said, "Yes. I see the tarp over them because light from the stars is so bright, they need a shade to block all the light."

He said, "Do you see the shape the sky filled with stars has formed? It's a bright, huge crucifix named *The Southern Cross*."

It was so beautiful and so restful. I remember from grammar school the teacher pointing it out to us in the encyclopedia while studying geography.

Tokyo Rose was no longer on the radio announcing propaganda to the troops in the Pacific. Someone on Manus wrote the song, *Rum and Coca-Cola*, which was frequently played over the airwaves.

The juke boxes held twenty records in taverns and many public places. They were filled with many of Frank Sinatra's records. We heard his singing over the radio on Manus. He was popular in the music circles, and a teen idol.

The guys spent a lot of time writing home. One bunk partner in our hut did more than anyone else. At times he asked us if his writing was any good. When I read what he wrote, I asked him to do a nice one I could mail home.

Two days later he surprised me with one scribbled on lined paper, and he said to me, "Here you are. You're an okay guy; hope you like it," and handed it to me. It was a good description of what some of our life was while living on Manus.

The Letter

Have you ever sat through a picture show, while rain seeped through your trousers, Joe?

Have you ever labored in mildewed clothes, or stepped on a lizard with your naked toes?

Have you ever stood until you thought you'd choke, in line for ice cream or a bottle of Coke, only to hear the familiar shout, "We're sorry guys, but we just ran out"?

To be just more specific, have you ever been in the South Pacific?

Have you ever weakened in a chilling fright, to some awesome sound of the tropic night?

Has your skin ever turned a yellow-green, from daily doses of Atabrine?

Has your sweat ever dripped on your writing pad, while you penned a letter to your mom and dad?

Have you ever been tempted to moan and sob, at the fate of a lonely gob?

Have you ever wished you could step down bare, and roll around

260

in the snow back there?

If you don't think that would be terrific, then you have never been in the South Pacific.

Have you ever thrilled to the symphony, of the gentle surf of an azure sea?

Have you ever sifted the coral sand, for the ocean jewels of this starred land?

Have you ever watched the moonlight trace, soft pattern of gold and silver lace?

Then you have never tasted the joys prolific, of the fabled islands of the South Pacific.

Have you ever stood on a jungle ridge, and yearned for the sight of the Golden Gate Bridge?

Would you trade any one of these fancied thrills, for a sunny hike in the Palos Hills, or a berry patch in the Carolines, or a hunter's shack in the northern pines?

Then just to be a bit more specific, you should be here in the South Pacific.

Only Two Were Made

They were small aircraft carriers. One was the Belleau Wood. One day in December, 1945, I took pictures of a ship that had a new, unusual design that caught my eye.

In the late afternoon, a boatswain of an LCM saw three of us lingering at the dock and asked if we cared to join him for a ride. It was to check out the performance of their boat's two engines that had just been serviced. We jumped aboard.

As we pulled out from the dock, right in the middle of the harbor was an aircraft carrier with a funny backside. I asked the driver to get close to it. He not only sailed close to it but also swung around the backside so I could take a picture. I felt good; I was glad I had my camera with me. We looked at it and our curiosity was satisfied, so we sailed out of the harbor.

He revved up the two engines to top speed. While enjoying our ride, the boatswain soon realized that we had gone too far out, and with the big waves we decided to go back.

As our boat turned around, one hollered out, "I see a small boat with a little white sail. It looks like a native's outrigger with a person on it." Evening was approaching, the waves were threatening, and that lone outrigger was far out on the ocean.

The boatswain said, "There's only enough fuel to return to shore. IF we help that guy, we might get into deep trouble, lost at sea." In a second, we voted to go get him. When we reached him, his makeshift sail was torn. He wore only shorts, no shirt, his body blue from the cold as he shivered. It was December; the monsoon winds were warning us.

As soon as our boat approached, he jumped aboard and crouched in a corner of the boat to be out of the wind.

We made an attempt to save his small boat from the water with the ramp, which should've dropped next to it. With the large waves, the boatswain couldn't control the heavy ramp and it fell on the boat, crushing it to pieces.

Returning to shore was worrisome, the fuel was very low. When we got to the dock, it felt like home (the fuel gauge flickered on E).

In August, 2009, I met Mike at a fish fry at the VFW in New Lenox. I was surprised to hear him say he served in the Navy during World War Two, and served on a ship in the Pacific on an aircraft carrier anchored in Seeadler Harbor outside Manus Island in December, 1945. He told me only two ships were built with that design, and he served on the Belleau Wood. The fantail was designed to serve and accommodate vessels at the ocean's water level.

That rang a bell. I had pictured of one of those that I shot with my bullet camera at the same place he described. I saw him at the next fish fry and showed him the pictures. He recognized them immediately and said, "That was the ship I was on."

His job was to prepare and assist aircraft to ascend to the flight deck for flight. He said the work he did was like working in the basement.

More About Manus Island

It is a part of Papua, New Guinea. Lorengau is the capitol. Seeadler Harbor is its front door.

Asylum-seekers have been released onto Manus from Australia between 2001 and 2004, and again from 2012 until August 17, 2016, when it was made illegal. On October 31, 2017, it was scheduled to close, and the Australian government granted over $56 million to the inmates.

Manus was first recorded as founded by Spanish explorers on August 15, 1528. It is the home of the Emerald Green Snail, whose shells are harvested to be sold as jewelry. We called them "cat-eyes." They are a beautiful shade of green and they are half-round, and a half-inch in size.

A few from our group searched for them in the coral areas of the oceanfront. One day, a guy told me he searched for them often but quit. I asked why. He said, "While poking with my knife in the coral's crevices, hoping to find some, a deadly coral snake popped out inches from my face, as if to say hello."

After living in the Admiralty Islands over a year, I had to review what I had learned about these natives.

A person who wears hardly any clothing, has very little property, and cannot read or write, has some capabilities and knowledge that I envy. They need no money to survive. Spear-fishing and hunting in the jungle is their expertise.

When I saw a man with his wife and two children in a

fifteen-foot outrigger take off from the shore in the dark of night, out into the ocean without life vests, I had to ask, what goes with them? One elderly man explained to me, "They are just going to visit some relative at some surrounding islands. They navigate by the stars, and by the currents during certain seasons. They will be okay."

They know the perils of the rivers and the ocean. A crocodile could turn their boat over in a second, or a barracuda, which can move at forty miles per hour, could attack at any time.

Some of the natives had neglected good health habits. Teens smoked and chewed betel nuts to get a high. Some had unattended sores and some women said they'd rather be pregnant often so not to bother with their monthly feminine body obligation. The children learned the ways of life early, and it was obvious. Some children learned to swim before they walked.

My Trip Home

USS Lauderdale

This was the ship that brought me and 1,914 other sailors gathered from other islands back to the United States. It was a troop transport ship, the USS Lauderdale (APA-179). It was one year old, and had only one 5.51" gun on its fantail. The ship's most useful purpose was to transport troops from the Pacific Islands battlefronts to hospital ships or home during 1945 and 1946. Our trip home was a part of the *Magic Carpet* movement.

Tickets were needed, and were printed out for each of us in order to board the ship. Pete, Spoony, Warner, Benjy and I walked up the plank together, showed our passes, and headed right to a chosen bunk below decks. I dropped my ditty bag on the cot and headed for chow. It was December 22, 1945, about 7 p.m. After chow we migrated around the gun on the fantail. We talked about how good we felt about getting on to our journey home. I said, "It felt like a removed a two-hundred-pound burden from my body." Others agreed.

As the sun crossed the horizon, our ship started the engines and we sailed out of Seeadler Harbor. I looked back, and all I saw were jungle tree tops.

We sailed northward, across the equator. On the third day, it was Christmas Eve. The ship's commander, W. F. Ramsey, gave us a holiday greeting over the speakers and we all said a prayer together before eating our turkey dinner. It had all the trimmings, just like home. Since we crossed the dateline, we gained a day so we ate turkey two days in a row.

The meals were excellent but the weather became very rough. Many meals were skipped on account of the rough seas we entered, which had rough waves. It rained continuously for about four days and then a solid fog formed ahead. I sheltered against a bulkhead most of that time. It was too warm to go below decks. The ship sounded the foghorn repeatedly along with the bell clanging continuously as we moved at a snail's pace. By noon the next day, the fog cleared but the ocean got very rough. The ship bounced up and down, wavering side to side at a list of about 25 degrees.

My good ol' buddy Bud said, "Let's go up front and get sprayed by the shower of ocean water scooped up by the bow." It was daring but we did it once. We knew a warning would be announced over the speakers any moment.

Afterwards, I realized we could've been washed overboard.

Hours later, the water leveled off and smooth sailing began with cooler air. We headed for Pearl Harbor and I thought it would be a stopping point before continuing to our destination. I was wrong. When we entered the harbor, the ship's captain sailed up right up to the sunken *USS Arizona*. It had protective buoy markers around it. We all crowded against the rail on the ship's port side and got a good look. Only whispers were heard during those several moments of sadness. That site will remain with me forever. It was a nice gesture by the captain to give us that short but special tour.

USS Arizona

Then we shot out of the harbor at full speed – 18 knots per hour. I thought we were bound for California as our home port. Again, I was wrong.

On January 3, 1946, we saw land at around noon. One guy recognized the shored on both sides of the very wide cove. It was the Puget Sound. Our ship moved right smack through the center of it very slowly for about an hour and finally docked. It was Bremerton, Washington. The air temperature was 18 degrees. I only had on a thin sweater, trousers and shoes. I was very cold coming directly from the equatorial climate.

As I stepped off the ship ladder's last step and my feet hit the ground, I kissed it and followed it with a few push-ups. It felt sooooo gooooood.

A Naval barracks building was right on the waterfront. It was warm in there. We were given liberty that same night, but few took advantage of it. Some who did left their valuables in my care – it was mostly money.

There was a scale in the hallway on the first floor of the building. Everyone who saw it weighed themselves. I weighed 118 pounds, but when I left California for overseas, I weighed 148 pounds. After weighing I felt strong, healthy, and happy. One guy I saw through the window knelt down and kissed the ground three times.

The next morning, a bus took us to Seattle's railroad station. We walked some of the hilly streets nearby until train time. Right at noon, we boarded one n the extreme northern route eastward to Chicago. All the cars had coach seating.

A few things stand out in my mind about that train ride. It started out with eight train cars filled with sailors. As men were dropped off along the way at their home stations, coached emptied out and were eliminated. As the train traveled through northern Minnesota, when I saw all those lakes, I understood why it was called *The Land of 10,000 Lakes.*

Soon, only four cars were occupied, as the men emptied at their stations. The conductor locked the empty cars. I was in the car behind the steam engine, which carried a happy, peaceful bunch of sailors. However, in the car behind us was an exuberantly happy bunch who drank and were rowdy all the way. They brawled and busted several windows of that car. It was too warm and they

271

wanted air. When the train stopped and waited for the signal to proceed to their home station two blocks away, seven men in that car did not stay. They jumped through those broken-out windows and ran across the tracks to their homes.

Then it was quiet, so we entered that emptied car. What we saw was a mess. Torn newspapers, empty liquor containers, and the conductor standing near us, shaking his head in disbelief.

The train got the green signal and we pulled into the station in the Twin Cities – Minneapolis-St. Paul. From there I rode to Chicago on the "Route of the 400" line, right into Union Station.

When I walked out of the station and to the street, the hustle and bustle of the people, auto horns, flickering lights and police-car horns blaring down the streets gripped me with joy so quickly that tears came from my eyes. To me it was like an amusement park. I was nearly home.

Neatly dressed in Navy uniform, carrying my small ditty bag, I proudly walked and occasionally jogged the who six blocks to the LaSalle Street station, and rode home on the Rock Island train.

When I got home, my mom was the first to see me and she cried, and my father smiled as we hugged. Everything got more cheerful when my three brothers entered the house to welcome me home.

I took my 30-day leave and then reported to Great Lakes Illinois Naval Training Center for my discharge.

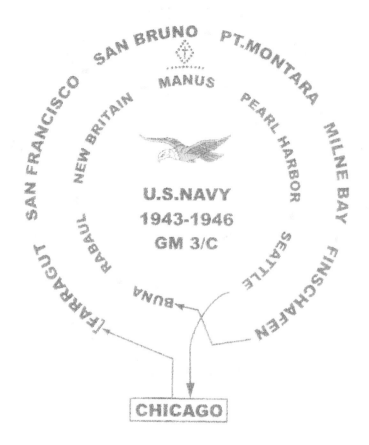

SAN BRUNO PT.MONTARA

MANUS

SAN FRANCISCO

NEW BRITAIN

PEARL HARBOR

MILNE BAY

U.S.NAVY
1943-1946
GM 3/C

SEATTLE

FINSCHAFEN

[FARRAGUT

RABAUL

BUNA

CHICAGO

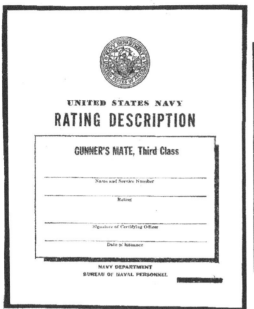

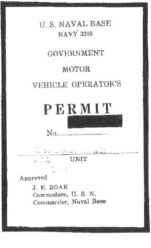

Maximum, 1 beer per day and wherever and when ever it was available.

There, we were told that processing papers for discharge would only take about an hour. Ho, ho, ho. After receiving them, we went our separate ways, and my heart softened as we said our goodbyes to each other.

Benjy said to me, "Someone is handing out flyers; take one."
The heading on it was *A Short Course to Rotation.*

Name:

Rate:

Serial no.:

Months overseas:

This application must be accompanied by your service jacket and proof card. With men now leaving our organization to return to the States, we have found from reports drifting back to us that these men are required to attend school for two weeks. The purpose of this school is to teach men culture and refinement in order that they may re-adapt themselves to the far gentler life in the States. The men are anxious to return home and a two-week delay for school is hard to take, so in order to remedy this, we compiled this pertinent data. After taking this short course, it will not be necessary to attend any school and you may go directly home, confident that you are able to mix with any groups, be it saloon or salon. This course has carried our seal of approval.

Excerpts From the Short Course

1. Upon arrival I America, you will be amazed at the large number of beautiful girls you will see. (Remember, boys, the city is not the jungle.) Many are very intelligent, and some are hair stylists, stenographers, teachers, and counter girls. Be polite and treat them right, as one may become your wife.
      In a restaurant when the waitress plops your bill

down on the table, the back side of it is not for your phone number. When you eat and leave, and she says, "You all come back again," it does not mean you answer, "What time do you get off?"

2. If you are visiting someone's home and spend the night there, you are awakened by a rap on the door informing you the household is rising, the proper answer is, "I'll be up shortly." DO not say, "Blow it out your royal ***."

3. The first meal in the morning being breakfast, you will find a strange assortment of foods, such as cantaloupe, fresh milk, homemade bread and some puddings. Don't be afraid to eat them; they are palatable. If you wish for the butter, you turn to the nearest person and say, "Would you please pass the butter," not, "Throw me the damn grease." Food is served in separate plates, milk is not called Cow Juice. You have been eating the beans mixed with pudding or gravy spread onto the cake which was your dessert. You do not have to guard your food with your elbows; no one will grab it. If you belch, don't say, "It must be the lousy chow, when does the good stuff come?"

4. If and when a biological urge comes upon you, the facilities to use may look strange to you. You do not carry your helmet just in case, or a shovel and a newspaper. Get acquainted with the facilities pointed out to you. The sink next to the latrine is for washing.

5. If you entertain, don't serve your guests such drinks as Raisin Jack, Reefer Fluid, or Coconut Wine. They will be poor company after two drinks. When being served champagne or a better drink you've never had, you do not snatch the bottle from them with a beastly loo and empty it with one long gulp. Don't bang a beer bottle on a table's edge to open it.

6. If someone has erred in some situation , politely correct them but don't say, "SNAFU, situation normal, all f***ed up."

7. When leaving company of someone's home and you cannot

find the apparel you came with, don't say, "Don't anybody leave, some S.O.B. got my coat and hat."

8. At movies, no more air raids. No helmet is needed Be mannered, don't whistle at every female walking down the aisle. If some in front are taller, "Move your head, jerk," is not polite, and when those near you whisper too loud, saying to them, "Nail it" might cause an upheaval, so be careful.

9. When shopping for civilian clothing, it will be a real problem. You will not find exactly what you want. The war caused a shortage and returning servicemen increased the demand, and production of manufacturing clothing has not caught up. In stores, you will many times say to the sales people, "You expect me to wear these?"

10. If all these suggestions and info fails you, the alternate solution is to consider this: re-enlist.

Back in Civvies

It was strange when I flopped back to this side of the world where I grew up. My habits hadn't changed but my mood did. One notable concern entered my mind. No more military or parental guidance. I was twenty-one years old and I would be responsible for my own actions.

When I stood on a train platform, waiting for transportation to work one day, I thought about it and my nerves jittered for a minute.

The following day, things disturbed me to a point where an argument erupted at home. My mother showed sadness as that happened, so the next day I called in sick at work and went down to Navy Pier, where Navy veterans received help with their problems. There, I explained my situation. I received a short, quick answer: A re-adjustment problem.

The assisting officer said, "After exercising your body you feel better, so exercise your mind, keep busy, and you will feel better, you will feel okay." I accepted that answer and followed that to this day. On that visit, I learned help was available for a whole year after the war for World War Two veterans.

Most of my friends did not wait long to marry. I liked beer, and the shuffleboard and pinball machines in local taverns. I browsed through taverns and bowling alleys almost every night until midnight for six months after my discharge.

I met up with my Navy buddies. We talked about military

service. Ernie, a swimming partner from high school was in the Army Air Corps, are in civilian life he became a flight engineer for American Airlines. Reno had been a radioman on the *USS New Jersey*, and back home he repaired TVs for a living. Joe was a baker on a destroyer, and when he was discharged, he operated a grocery store. Alex served on an aircraft carrier as an electrician, and became an engineer at a steel mill. Jimmy was a carpenter in the Navy and he would up working in the building construction industry. Bob, who served at a Naval air station office, got his job back at the Rock Island railroad engineering office as a draftsman – along with me.

My friend Alfred (Alphy) was different. He grew up on the next street from me. We played together a lot. I had one problem that irked me. Often when I knocked on his door to ask for him to come out and play, his mom most always answered, "He is practicing his violin lessons," or "He is doing his homework." For two hours? That much?

I thought I was the winner. Well, who was the winner? I left the Navy with the rank of a third-class petty officer. After he served, his rank was Rear Admiral.

Years Went By

As time went by, webs connected my Navy life. A few were great surprises. While I lived in Missouri during the '80s and '90s, I visited my family and friends in Illinois. During one visit, I bunked at my son Jim's house in Oak Forest. His family and I attended church services on Saturday evenings.

This one time before going to church, Jim said, "Dad, I will have you meet someone you may or may not know after services." I told him I did not understand his meaning. He answered, That's okay. You'll know what I mean when you meet him." Off to church we went.

After services, as the crowd flowed out the doors, Jim pulled a man aside and said, "I want you to meet my dad."

As soon as he heard that, he gripped me lime a magnet and repeated to me at least ten times, "Thank you, thank you."

The man was an American missionary who schooled natives on Manus, before and during the time when the Japanese held the island. My thoughts bled when that missionary said, "The Japanese bayonets were just yards away from me and my associates as we hid in the jungle. Suddenly, the firing of American rifles was heard, and that saved us. You guys came just in time." We talked a lot and he repeated to me, "Thank you, thank you."

After many years, another surprise meeting occurred around 2010. It happened in New Lenox at St. Jude's church. At

FLAG of MANUS

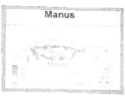

beginning of Mass one Saturday evening, a missionary dressed in his white priest's garb walked down the aisle to the altar. He conducted the entire service beautifully. Judging by his sermon, I thought he was very well educated, but where did he come from? Believe it or not, he came from the Great Britain province in the Pacific Ocean, which covers the Admiralty Islands – mainly Manus, the capitol.

As the crowd gathered around him in the narthex after service, he performed a native dance while waving a jiggler in the air and then told some stories to those standing around him.

I asked him to pose for some pictures. He did, and we talked about Manus Island. I offered to send a donation to his home address. He said, "No, no, do not do that." That surely surprised me. He explained to me how disorganized and unsettled the situation was in the island area. Mail was redirected by certain unscrupulous individuals to be used for their own benefit. "I would never receive your mail," he said. After we talked about the tremendous change taking place in the Admiralty Islands, he departed to his next mission.

As the years passed, my life slipped by very fast as I bounced around from one job to another. I finally settled down at my last place of employment, at the steel mill, until retirement at the age of 62.

A few days before retirement, a phone repairman came into my office and made wiring changes. He looked about my age, so I asked him if he was in the service during World War Two. He said, "Yes, I was an electrician in the Navy on the *USS Iowa*." I asked if he sailed near Manus, but he said, "No."

The next day a different man came to complete work on the phone wiring. He also appeared to be my age and I asked if he served in World War Two. He said, "Yes, I was a pilot of a P-38 fighter plane."

I asked, "Did you fly in the Pacific area?"

He said, "Yes, in several invasions."

"How about Manus Island?"

He said, "I was in the mission that attacked Los Negros and Manus Islands during that invasion."

His eyes lit up as he bragged about how well his plane performed while he flew it, but he said, "It had one fault." While describing to me with hand motions, he said, "When turning the plane to the left, there was one blind spot at the right rear of the one fuselage that was a concern during combat. I had to keep that constantly in mind."

In Conclusion

This book contains pictures, Illustrations and stories with some descriptions of actual incidents that occurred during my thirty months of service in the United States Navy during World War Two. Our military struggled through many things with vast amounts of endurance. I can only take a very minute amount of credit on my part compared to all those injured or lost in combat as part of winning the greatest war in history.

So many times I had frightening moments and faced unpredictable situations we encountered at hand. It was so often that the body and mind were strained so tremendously, far beyond the zone of comfort. It was very difficult, but I am very proud of our success in enduring and completing those many accomplishments without regret.

The operation of explosives handling began with a combination of ninety gunners and torpedomen at Lugos Mission on Manus Island, and enlarged to a total of 177 by the time it was at full operation, once the entire four echelons entered our work force.

It has changed the direction and future of my life in a way I would have never anticipated. I was definitely impacted.

Commander Cunneen, who was in charge at the beginning, gave us direction in getting a foothold of the primary operations in handling the ammunition used by the ships and troops in fighting the enemy. A meritorious award was applied to each of our records by him.

The next commander, Jones, who followed and supervised us through the most hectic part of all our services to war's end, also awarded us with a written commendation in our records for our tiring efforts, without stop, through those difficult times.

My friend Paul had a plaque of Lion Four mounted, with his war souvenirs, in the Nimitz Museum in Fredericksburg, Texas, which is visited by thousands each year.

LION 4 - NAVY 3205

ADMIRALTY ISLANDS

PLAQUE DEDICATION CEREMONY
LION 4 - NAVY 3205

ADMIRAL NIMITZ MUSEUM
FREDERICKSBURG, TEXAS
AUGUST 30, 1996

LION 4-NAVY 3205
ADMIRALTY ISLANDS
World War II–Pacific Theater
1944-1946

Kali Bay

MANUS ISLAND

Los Negros
Island

Dedicated to all who served
in the Admiralty Islands

and in remembrance of comrades who
have since passed away

We Shall Never Forget

Presented by the families and former shipmates
who remain united by the bonds of comradeship
August 30, 1996

My most honorable mention is in the Congressional Record at the 105th Congress in Washington, DC, at the second session, which included all 177 of our Lion Four group. And as you will see, even with such an honor, they still spelled my name wrong:

Congressional Record

PROCEEDINGS AND DEBATES OF THE 105th CONGRESS

SECOND SESSION

HONORING MEMBERS OF THE LION 4 UNIT OF WORLD WAR II

HON. HOWARD COBLE OF NORTH CAROLINA
IN THE HOUSE OF REPRESENTATIVES
Monday, June 22, 1998

Mr. COBLE: Mr. Speaker, I would like to take this opportunity to recognize a little-known, but immensely significant, group that valiantly served our country in World War II. This heroic group of individuals, members of the "Lion 4" unit, served to supply and repair the many needs of the huge Navy presence in the Pacific theater. This unit, along with the other brave soldiers who fought the war in the Pacific, helped us defeat the Japanese and end the war months earlier than expected. We shall never forget the accomplishments of these men, some of America's true heroes. The Lion 4 unit landed on the Admiralty Islands north of New Guinea, with the daunting task of having to build a base equal to Pearl Harbor in size and function, with room to anchor over 400 ships. They landed on February 29, 1944, and by March 10, a severely damaged airfield was operational, providing pivotal air support during the war. Amazingly, at least 36 major units were operational by July, merely five months after the Lion 4 had first landed! These men had almost single-handedly created the largest and most important naval and air base in the Pacific Theatre. This in spite of knee-deep mud, torrential rainfall, 120-degree temperatures, malaria, and the constant risk of death from the ongoing war around them. They built this base so that the fighting troops could get supplies and repairs, and the time saved, in addition to the Lion 4's service, served to cut short the war and break the back of the Japanese

287

forces. On behalf of the men and women of the Sixth District of North Carolina, we proudly honor these men for their service to our country. The following men, members of Lion Four/ Navy 3205 Association, are among the servicemen who helped keep our country free and proud: Marlen Adrian, Albert Aguero, Edwin Anguiski, Robert Archer, Ford Basel, Leonard Bearce, Ralph Benavidez, S.Q. Berry, Donald Berry, Henry J. Bozenski, Donald Bratt, Robert Bridges, Robert Bridges, George Briggs, Ernest Brown, Harold Brown, Williams Burg, Lenard Callaway, Loran Cambell, Pat Cannavino, Harold Cazaubon, Morris J. Coe, Marion Cook, George Crosley, Jesse Daniels, Carrol Day, Fred Defield, Martin Delozier, John Dick, Augustine DiSano, Malone Downes, Irvine Downs, Earl Dressen, Robert Dunn, Frank Durbin, James Eby, Carl Eitel, Max Ellis, Howard Espenson, Joseph Frendling, D.P. Garner, Shelton Gautreaux, William Gaydos, George Gerberding, John Geschrey, John Glaser, Charles Granger, Chester Grobschmidt, Sam Guerrero, Frank Halder, E. Lee Hall, Garry Hanson, Robert Hartigan, Robert Harwood, Thomas Hatcher, Ralph Hayes, George Haymes, James Heand, Robert Heeke, Charles Heiss, Forrest Herron, Jr., John Herzog, Preston Hoalst, Frank Hogan, Charles Hoggatt, Douglas Hood, Kenneth Hoyt, William Hutchison, Joe Jacob, Clifford James, James Jensen, Farris Jobe, Hal Johnson, **Sylvester Kapoclus**, James Kauffman, Eugene Kennedy, Chester Kershner, Andrew Kube, Herman Kuhns, Robert Laflame, Marshall Leach, Bernard Lease, Marvin Leasure, Larry Leonard, Arthur Ludwig, Daniel Lukach, Paul Mahan, Charles Majewski, Perry Martin, Ken Mathews, William Maxwell, Charles McCabe, Eugene McCardell, Joseph Melillo, Jake Miller, Thomas Miller, Frank Moesher, Lawrence Moon, Dale Mulholand, Miles Mutchler, Evan Nardone, Glen Nelson, Donald Nephew, John Newkirk, William O'Dea, Howard Olson, Richard Ostrem, James Owens, lngert Pederson, James Pennebaker, Walter Pensak, Robert Phipps, William Piper, Donald Pittelko, I.C. Plaza, Marvin Plunkett, Floyd Prater, Melvin Rabbitt, Douglas Ragsdale, Al Raiola, George Roe, Robert Rosenburg, lrven Rustad, John Ruth, Paul Sanders, John Sarbach, Alvin Saxton, Roland Schomer, Oron Schuch, Carl Schultz, Robert Schultz, Harold Schwocho, Eldon Shomo, Paul Siler, Roy Smith, Ruben Stahl, C. Stewart, Wm. Stiffler, Phillip Storm, Robert Stower, John Streicher, Buford Swartwood, Robert Tafel, Louis Tangney, Ernest Taube, Lowell Ter Barch, John Thomas, Ronald Trabucco, Walker Treadway, Joshua Treat Ill, Robert Trevorah, Frank Van Poppelen, John Van Soest, Charles Vicory, John Ward, Chuck Washner, Harry Waugh, William

Webb, Harry Weiss, Hal Wenick, B.F. Williams, Sherwood Williams, Loren Yates, and Frank Zehner. Family members will be representing the following deceased members of Lion 4 at the next gathering in Williamsburg, Virginia: Herbert Banning, Edward Boyle, Mr. Daningger, Brayn Driggers, Thomas Hutchison, Bert Lancaster, Robert Riehm, Eugene Rushing, Arthur Schussler, Arnold Vann, Donald Williams, Edward Winikaitis, and Glen Zunke. As we sit here today, a half century after World War II, the need remains to honor those brave men and women who secured our freedom. On behalf of the citizens of the Sixth District of North Carolina, we express our deepest gratitude to the members of Lion Four and all the units that helped keep America free; we shall never forget their sacrifices.

Lastly – my camera. So many of my experiences are real because of this little guy:

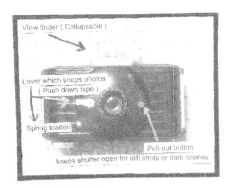

BULLET CAMERA $ 1:00

Camera size 4 3/4 " x 2 1/2 " x 1 1/2 "
Made by Eastman Kodak
Film roll had 8 frames
Negative size 1 1/4 " x 1 5/8 "
Shutter speed 1/100 of a second
In 1938 roll of standard film cost 25 cents,
Super film 30 cents.

View finder (Collapsable)
Lever which snaps photos (Push down type)
Spring loaded
Pull-out button
keeps shutter open for still shots or dark scenes

Telescope (Twirls in and out)

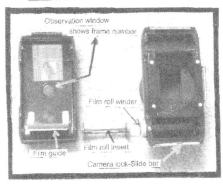

Observation window
shows frame number
Film roll winder
Film roll insert
Film guide
Camera lock-Slide bar

A negative would enlarge an 8 " x 10 " photo with an unoticeable amount of resolution loss.

Made in the USA
Monee, IL
17 December 2023